How **NOT** to **KILL** Your Houseplant

How **NOT** to **KILL** Your Houseplant

Survival Tips for the Horticulturally Challenged

Veronica Peerless

CONTENTS

Find your plant   4

THE BASICS   12
Buy it   14
Pot it & place it   16
Water it   18
Feed it & love it   20
Repot it   22
Plant pests   24
Plant diseases   28

THE HOUSEPLANTS   30

With specific care details for 114
different plants, this section provides
all the information you need to treasure
your houseplant and troubleshoot
any problems.

TOP 5 PLANTS FOR
Your desk   46
Sunny spots   66
The bathroom   86
Low light   106
Your living room   126

Index   140
Author & acknowledgments   143
Toxicity   143

FIND YOUR PLANT

URN PLANT
Aechmea fasciata
pp.32–33

FLAMING SWORD
Vriesea splendens
p.33

GUZMANIA
Guzmania lingulata
p.33

LIPSTICK PLANT
Aeschynanthus pulcher
pp.34–35

AGAVE
Agave
p.39

ASPARAGUS FERN
Asparagus setaceus
p.43

PAINTED-LEAF BEGONIA
Begonia rex
p.45

FISHBONE CACTUS
Disocactus anguliger
p.35

HAWORTHIA
Haworthia
p.39

EMERALD FERN
Asparagus densiflorus
Sprengeri Group
p.43

QUEEN'S TEARS
Billbergia nutans
pp.48–49

ELEPHANT'S EAR
Alocasia x amazonica
pp.36–37

FLAMINGO FLOWER
Anthurium
pp.40–41

POLKA-DOT BEGONIA
Begonia maculata
pp.44–45

PINK QUILL
Tillandsia cyanea
p.49

ALOE VERA
Aloe vera
pp.38–39

FOXTAIL FERN
Asparagus densiflorus
'Myersii'
pp.42–43

ELIATOR HYBRIDS
Begonia Eliator Group
p.45

BLUSHING BROMELIAD
Neoregelia carolinae
f. tricolor
p.49

continued

PEACOCK PLANT
Calathea
pp.50–51

POTHOS
Epipremnum
p.53

STRING OF BEADS
Senecio rowleyanus
p.57

FLORISTS' CYCLAMEN
Cyclamen persicum
pp.60–61

PRAYER PLANT
Maranta
p.51

GRAPE IVY
Cissus rhombifolia
p.53

HEARTS ON A STRING
Ceropegia woodii
p.57

INDOOR AZALEA
Rhododendron simsii
p.61

STROMANTHE
Stromanthe
p.51

NATAL LILY
Clivia miniata
pp.54–55

NEVER-NEVER PLANT
Ctenanthe burle-marxii
pp.58–59

DIEFFENBACHIA
Dieffenbachia seguine
pp.62–63

CURLY SPIDER PLANT
Chlorophytum comosum
'Bonnie'
pp.52–53

MONEY PLANT
Crassula ovata
pp.56–57

CROTON
Codiaeum variegatum
p.59

ARROWHEAD PLANT
Syngonium podophyllum
p.63

SHAMROCK PLANT
Oxalis triangularis
p. 63

DRACAENA COMPACTA
Dracaena fragrans
pp. 68–69

HEN & CHICKS
Echeveria
pp. 72–73

FIDDLE-LEAF FIG
Ficus lyrata
pp. 76–77

VENUS FLY TRAP
Dionaea muscipula
pp. 64–65

DRACAENA MARGINATA
Dracaena marginata
p. 69

AEONIUM
Aeonium
p. 73

WEEPING FIG
Ficus benjamina
p. 77

PITCHER PLANT
Sarracenia
p. 65

SONG OF INDIA
Dracaena reflexa
p. 69

TIGER'S JAW
Faucaria
p. 73

RUBBER PLANT
Ficus elastica
p. 77

MONKEY CUPS
Nepenthes
p. 65

LUCKY BAMBOO
Dracaena sanderiana
pp. 70–71

POINSETTIA
Euphorbia pulcherrima
pp. 74–75

NERVE PLANT
Fittonia
pp. 78–79

continued

PURPLE PASSION
Gynura aurantiaca
p.79

JAPANESE ARALIA
Fatsia japonica
p.81

BUTTERFLY PALM
Dypsis lutescens
p.85

CALANDIVA
Kalanchoe
Calandiva® Series
p.91

POLKA-DOT PLANT
Hypoestes
p.79

AMARYLLIS
Hippeastrum
pp.82–83

WAX FLOWER
Hoya carnosa
pp.88–89

CROCODILE FERN
Microsorum musifolium
pp.92–93

ENGLISH IVY
Hedera helix
pp.80–81

KENTIA PALM
Howea fosteriana
pp.84–85

MINIATURE WAX PLANT
Hoya bella
p.89

BOSTON FERN
Nephrolepis exaltata
'Bostoniensis'
pp.93

SPOTTED LAUREL
Aucuba japonica
p.81

PARLOUR PALM
Chamaedorea elegans
p.85

FLAMING KATY
Kalanchoe blossfeldiana
pp.90–91

BIRD'S NEST FERN
Asplenium nidus
p.93

SENSITIVE PLANT
Mimosa pudica
pp. 94–95

BUNNY EARS CACTUS
Opuntia microdasys
pp. 98–99

CREEPING BUTTONS
Peperomia rotundifolia
p. 101

IMPERIAL RED PHILODENDRON
Philodendron 'Imperial Red'
pp. 108–109

SPLIT-LEAF PHILODENDRON
Monstera deliciosa
pp. 96–97

MONK'S HOOD
Astrophytum ornatum
p. 99

RAINDROP PEPEROMIA
Peperomia polybotrya
p. 101

HEART-LEAF PHILODENDRON
Philodendron scandens
p. 109

XANADU PHILODENDRON
Thaumatophyllum xanadu
p. 97

CROWN CACTUS
Rebutia
p. 99

MOTH ORCHID
Phalaenopsis
pp. 102–103

BLUSHING PHILODENDRON
Philodendron erubescens
p. 109

SWISS CHEESE VINE
Monstera adansonii
p. 97

WATERMELON PEPEROMIA
Peperomia argyreia
pp. 100–101

BLUE STAR FERN
Phlebodium aureum
pp. 104–105

MISSIONARY PLANT
Pilea peperomioides
pp. 110–111

continued

FRIENDSHIP PLANT
Pilea involucrata
'Moon Valley'
p.111

AFRICAN VIOLET
Saintpaulia
pp.114–115

FOOTSTOOL PALM
Saribus rotundifolius
pp.118–119

ZEBRA PLANT
Aphelandra squarrosa
p.121

ALUMINUM PLANT
Pilea cadierei
p.111

SNAKE PLANT
Sansevieria trifasciata
pp.116–117

FISH-TAIL PALM
Caryota mitis
p.119

CHRISTMAS CACTUS
Schlumbergera buckleyi
pp.122–123

ELKHORN FERN
Platycerium bifurcatum
pp.112–113

AFRICAN SPEAR
Sansevieria cylindrica
p.117

PYGMY DATE PALM
Phoenix roebelenii
p.119

EASTER CACTUS
Schlumbergera gaetneri
p.123

REGAL ELKHORN FERN
Platycerium grande
p.113

AFRICAN MILK BUSH
Euphorbia trigona
p.117

UMBRELLA TREE
Schefflera arboricola
pp.120–121

MISTLETOE CACTUS
Rhipsalis baccifera
p.123

PEACE LILY
Spathiphyllum
pp.124–125

CAPE PRIMROSE
Streptocarpus
pp.130–131

FLAME NETTLE
Solenostemon
p.135

ZZ PLANT
Zamioculcas zamiifolia
pp.138–139

CHINESE EVERGREEN
Aglaonema
p.125

GLOXINIA
Sinningia speciosa
p.131

YUCCA
Yucca elephantipes
pp.136–137

SAGO PALM
Cycas revoluta
p.139

CAST IRON PLANT
Aspidistra eliator
p.125

AIR PLANTS
Tillandsia
pp.132–133

TI PLANT
Dracaena angustifolia
p.137

GUINEA CHESTNUT
Pachira aquatica
p.139

BIRD OF PARADISE
Strelitzia reginae
pp.128–129

INCH PLANT
Tradescantia zebrina
pp.134–135

PONYTAIL PALM
Beaucarnea recurvata
p.137

THE
BASICS

**WHAT EVERY HOUSEPLANT
NEEDS TO STAY ALIVE**

BUY IT

If possible, buy your houseplant from a nursery or garden center, where it will have been properly cared for. Here are a few things to consider when choosing a houseplant, including how to get it home without killing it!

SHAPE

Ensure that the plant has a good shape. Look for bushy plants, and avoid those that are leggy or spindly.

Dieffenbachia
(pp.62–63)

POTTING MIX

Test the potting mix to see if it's moist. It shouldn't be soggy or very dry, as these are signs that the plant may not have been watered correctly.

ROOTS

If there are lots of roots visible on top of the potting mix and underneath the bottom of the pot, the plant is pot-bound (or root-bound). Avoid these plants as they will have been struggling to thrive and so won't be in peak condition.

FLOWERING PLANTS

When choosing a flowering plant, make sure it has both flowers and buds. Plants with buds will last longer because these buds will open and replace older, fading flowers. Avoid plants with only tightly closed buds, as these may not open when you get the plant home.

Pot mum

WRAP IT UP

Spring or summer is the best time to buy a houseplant, as the weather is often milder and the plant won't be too "shocked" by the sudden change in temperature and location. If you are buying a plant in winter when it is cold, be sure to wrap it up when taking it home, as the sudden change in temperature can cause the buds or leaves to fall off some plants, or even kill others. Poinsettias are particularly vulnerable to the cold.

CONDITION

Check that the leaves are fresh and have a good color, with no signs of browning or yellowing.

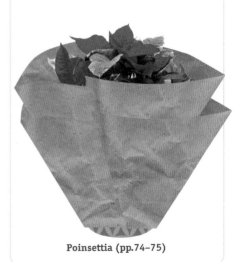

Poinsettia (pp.74–75)

PESTS & DISEASES

Look for signs of pests or diseases, making sure to check the undersides of the leaves (see Plant pests, pp.24–27, and Plant diseases, pp.28–29).

POT IT & PLACE IT

Once you get your houseplant home, you'll need to check that your plant is in a pot with drainage holes, and find a suitable location for it. Doing these two things will go a long way toward helping you keep it healthy.

HOW TO POT IT

Most houseplants come in plastic pots with drainage holes in the bottom. You can put these inside more ornamental pots. Some plants are sold in ornamental pots with no drainage holes. This makes it difficult to judge whether water is gathering at the bottom of the pot and rotting the roots. It's best to repot these plants into a plastic pot with drainage holes —this could be a plastic pot that you hide within a more attractive one.

Dieffenbachia (pp.62–63)

Ensure that the plastic pot fits into the pot you want to use

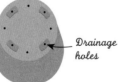

Drainage holes

PLANTS SOLD IN PLASTIC POTS
Check to see if your plant is in a pot with drainage holes at the bottom.

REPOTTING INTO A PLASTIC POT
If your plant is sold in only an ornamental pot, repot it into a plastic pot with drainage holes before concealing it in an ornamental container.

WHERE TO PUT IT

To find the right spot for your plant, think about temperature, light, and humidity. **Research where it hails from originally**—plants native to the rainforest floor won't enjoy a sun-baked windowsill. Check your plant's needs and put it in a place that suits it, not you.

TEMPERATURE

Most houseplants enjoy the same conditions we do—warm during the day, and cooler at night. Some plants, such as ivy and cyclamen, prefer lower temperatures. Houseplants do not enjoy significant fluctuations in temperature, so avoid the following places:

→ Near a heat register
→ Near an air-conditioning vent
→ In drafts
→ On a windowsill, behind curtains at night

You could use a thermometer to check room temperature

LIGHT

Light is a houseplant's source of energy, and some plants need more light than others. Most houseplants do well in bright, indirect or filtered light, out of direct sunlight. They are usually best placed around 12–35in (30–90cm) away from a north-, east-, or west-facing window. Keep in mind that the light can change during the course of the day, and at different times of year.

Aloe vera (pp.38–39)

HUMIDITY

Many houseplants originate from humid, tropical regions, and although they can cope with lower humidity, they may struggle in excessively hot or centrally heated rooms. Choose plants that originate from more arid environments, such as cacti and succulents, for rooms that are always dry. Keep more tropical plants away from direct sources of heat, such as space heaters, and consider moving them to a cooler or more humid room, such as a bathroom or kitchen. In warmer months, open a window: outdoor air is more humid than indoor. Some plants, such as ferns, are suited to the moist environment of a terrarium. Misting plants or placing them on a tray of pebbles filled with water used to be common advice for raising the humidity around plants, but this is now thought to have only a very limited, short-term effect.

Boston fern (p.93)

Parlor palm (p.85)

Kentia palm (pp.84–85)

WATER IT

Incorrect watering is the main reason that houseplants die—particularly overwatering. Here are the best methods to water healthy plants and save wilted ones.

HOW TO WATER IT

Most plants can be watered from above, but if your plant has hairy leaves or the foliage covers the potting mix, water from below to avoid splashing the leaves. Orchids can be dipped and drained—it allows their coarse soil to absorb the right amount of water. Water your plants with lukewarm water so that the temperature doesn't shock them. It's also worth leaving a bucket outside (if possible) to collect rainwater: some plants, such as bromeliads and carnivorous plants, prefer it, as they are sensitive to chemicals in hard tap water. Always remove the plant from its pot cover or dish before watering to keep it from sitting in water.

FROM ABOVE

For most plants, use a thin, long-necked watering can so that the spout can reach the potting mix easily. Water around the base of the plant so that the mix is evenly moist, and allow the excess water to drain away.

Dieffenbachia (pp.62–63)

FROM BELOW

Use this method to avoid splashing the leaves, which will create ugly marks and lead to the leaves rotting. Set the pot in a dish of water for around 30 minutes. Drain any excess water from the dish.

Cyclamen (pp.60–61)

DIP & DRAIN

A good technique for watering orchids: place the pot in a container of lukewarm water and leave it to stand for around 10 minutes. Let it drain thoroughly.

Moth orchid (pp.102–103)

HOW MUCH WATER?

Here are some things to consider when figuring out whether your plant needs watering, and how much water to give it.

→ **Overwatering combined with low light levels** is the number-one cause of houseplant death. The more light a plant gets, the more water it needs.

→ **Don't water on a fixed schedule**—get to know your plant's needs instead. Most plants only need watering when the top ½–¾in (1-2cm) of potting mix is dry—gently poke your finger into the soil to test it. If a rosette of leaves is covering the mix, go by the weight of the pot—a very light pot will have dry mix.

→ **Aim to make the potting mix moist**, but not wet. Most houseplants hate sitting in soggy potting mix, so always let excess water drain away.

→ **Potting mix in terra-cotta pots dries out more quickly** than that in plastic or ceramic pots; this is because terra-cotta is a porous material.

→ **Most plants need less water in the winter** because they are not actively growing. Some plants need this period of winter rest to reflower.

WILTING DUE TO UNDERWATERING?

If your plant has wilted, it may be due to a lack of water. Check that the potting mix is dry to confirm that your plant has been underwatered, as overwatering can have the same effect.

🔅 **SAVE IT** *Move your plant somewhere shady and fill a bowl with lukewarm water. In just its plastic pot with drainage holes, dunk your plant into the water, weighing it down if it floats. Soak for around 30 minutes and drain. The plant should revive within an hour.*

Peace lily
(pp.124–125)

WILTING DUE TO OVERWATERING?

Plants can also wilt due to waterlogging. This is much more serious; it can kill your plant more quickly than underwatering.

🔅 **SAVE IT** *Remove your plant from its pot(s) and wrap the root ball with newspaper or paper towels, replacing them until they have soaked up all the moisture. Repot the plant into fresh potting mix and keep the plant out of direct sun. Keep the mix just moist for a few weeks.*

Remove your plant from both its pots

African violet
(pp.114–115)

FEED IT & LOVE IT

You need to do more than just water your plant to keep it alive—most plants need feeding, too. It's also worth spending a few minutes each week examining and grooming your plant—it will thrive on your attention.

FEEDING

All plants need food to thrive. Carnivorous plants capture prey to feed on, but most houseplants will need a liquid houseplant feed. You should start feeding your plant a few weeks after you get it home, or around a couple of months after it has been repotted. In the spring and summer, add a liquid houseplant fertilizer to your watering can— usually around once a month. Be sure to follow the manufacturer's instructions and don't be tempted to add extra—overfeeding can damage the plant. It's best to feed when the potting mix is already moist—that way it will reach the roots directly and won't drain away. Alternatively, add slow-release pellets or spikes to the mix as a more low-maintenance approach—they'll release a little food every time you water. Don't feed houseplants in winter, unless they are winter-flowering.

Dwarf umbrella tree (pp.120–121)

Add liquid fertilizer to the water

Add fertilizer pellets to the potting mix

EXTRA CARE

Get to know your plant by spending a minute or two every week examining it and making sure it looks good. This is not only an important way to keep it healthy, but will mean you'll spot signs of problems more quickly when they occur.

GROOMING

Remove old leaves and deadhead flowers—this will encourage more blooms and will prevent dead petals from landing on the foliage, causing leaves to rot.

Remove old, brown leaves

Dracaena (pp.68–69)

CLEANING

Wipe your plant's leaves (especially those with large leaves) with a clean, damp cloth to keep them dust-free, as dust can keep light from getting to the leaves. Set palms in a lukewarm shower in winter, or a rain shower in summer. Fuzzy-leaved or prickly plants are best cleaned with a soft paintbrush.

Use a paintbrush for fuzzy leaves

Use a damp cloth to wipe waxy leaves

INSPECTING

Prevention is better than cure. If you notice that your plant is looking sickly, check your care regimen and look for signs of pests or diseases before they have a chance to cause significant problems (see Plant pests, pp.24–27, & Plant diseases, pp.28–29).

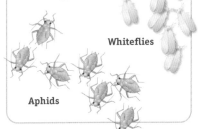

Whiteflies

Aphids

REPOT IT

Sooner or later, your plant's original potting mix will be exhausted, so your plant will need repotting. Chances are that the plant will have grown, too, so the plant will need repotting into a slightly larger pot.

WHEN TO REPOT

Most plants need repotting when their roots are curling around the edge of the potting mix; carefully remove the root ball to check. When repotting, choose a pot that's only slightly larger than the previous one—an extra 2in (5cm) in diameter is about right. A much larger pot will house too much mix and get waterlogged. Most plants are happy in peat-free houseplant or potted plant mix, but some, such as orchids and cacti, need a specialized mix. Do not use garden soil. The best time to repot is spring or summer. Some plants can look a little unhappy shortly after repotting, but they should recover—just continue to care for them as normal.

Fresh potting mix

PLANTS IN SMALLER POTS
Repot smaller plants into a new, larger pot, with fresh potting mix.

PLANTS IN LARGE POTS
It can be hard to take large, mature plants out of their containers, so "top dress" them instead. Remove the top 2–3in (5–8cm) of potting mix with a small trowel or spoon (take care not to damage roots) and replace it with fresh mix.

Dieffenbachia (pp.62–63)

Roots coming out of the bottom of the plant pot

Fiddle-leaf fig (pp.76–77)

HOW TO REPOT

Follow the steps to repot your plant correctly. You will need a new pot and fresh potting mix.

1 Water your plant the day before you repot it. It will be easier to remove and less likely to be "shocked" by repotting.

2 Add fresh potting mix to the base of the new, slightly larger pot.

3 Holding your plant upside down around the base of the stems, tap it out of its pot.

6 Water your plant, allowing any excess to drain away.

Leave 1in (2–3cm) at the top of the pot

4 Set your plant in the new pot. Leave space between the surface of the potting mix and the top of the pot.

5 Add potting mix around the root ball, firming it in gently.

"After repotting your plant, continue to care for it as normal."

PLANT PESTS

Houseplants can be troubled by small, unwelcome guests that can damage and even kill them.
Here's how to identify the signs of a pest infestation, and what you can do to save your plant.

HOW TO STOP PESTS

The best way to avoid pests is to keep your plant healthy, because healthy plants are better able to withstand a pest attack.

Check a plant over for signs of pests before buying, and check them regularly thereafter.

If your plant does become infected with a pest, you can try treating it with an environmentally friendly, nontoxic organic insecticide, such as an insecticidal or horticultural soap solution.

If you have a lot of houseplants in one place that are all suffering from the same problem, you could try a biological control. These natural products are available by mail order and work by introducing predators (usually invisible to the naked eye) to attack the pests.

Sticky trap

Begonia (pp.44–45)

Key
Where you will find the pests on your plants

Buds & stems   On the leaves   In the soil

"Healthy plants are better able to withstand a pest attack."

THE PESS

You may find signs of these pests on your houseplants. Plants that are particularly prone to infestation will have more details on their care page.

LEAF MINERS

Look for brown, white, or opaque meandering trails on the leaves, where the grubs have "mined" them. There may also be white dots on the leaves.

☀ TREAT IT *Remove the affected leaves. Spray with an organic insecticide.*

The grub tunnels through the layers of the leaf

Mum leaf

WHITEFLIES

They hide on the undersides of leaves, and clouds of tiny white insects will fly up when your plant is disturbed.

☀ TREAT IT *Temporarily move your plant outdoors and dislodge the insects with a spray of water. Also try hanging a sticky trap near the plant, which will take out large numbers of insects.*

Begonia leaf

THRIPS

Also known as thunder flies, these tiny brown or black sap-sucking insects may be seen on plants that have spent time outdoors. Signs of infestation include dull, mottled leaves, silvery-white streaks on the leaves or flowers, and distorted growth.

☀ TREAT IT *Sticky traps—especially blue ones—can reduce their numbers and can help you monitor the problem. Spray your plant with organic insecticide or try a biological control.*

FUNGUS GNATS

Also known as sciarid flies, these tiny brown or black insects fly around the plant. They aren't too harmful, but they are annoying. Their maggots mostly feed on organic matter in the potting mix, but can sometimes attack roots. Healthy plants can withstand this, but young or weak ones won't.

☀ TREAT IT *Allow the top ½–¾in (1–2cm) of potting mix to dry out before watering—they are attracted to wet soil. Make sure the plant has good light. A yellow sticky trap will attract the insects away from your plant. Cover the surface of the potting mix with a mulch of fine gravel or pebbles to prevent the gnats from laying their eggs.*

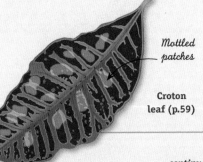

Mottled patches

Croton leaf (p.59)

continued

SPIDER MITES

Look for bleached or speckled foliage, webbing between the leaves and stems, and leaf fall. If you look under the leaves with the aid of a magnifying glass, you'll see the mites. Spider mites thrive in hot, dry conditions.

❤️ **TREAT IT** *Spray the whole plant with an organic insecticide or use a biological control. Be vigilant—use a magnifying glass to look for the mites on the underside of leaves.*

English ivy leaf (pp.80–81)

"Inspect your plant
regularly and deal
with problems before
they escalate."

VINE WEEVILS

If your plant has collapsed and you haven't over- or underwatered it, vine weevil grubs could be the culprit. They're found in the potting mix of plants that have spent time outside. They munch on the plant's roots, bulb, or tuber, causing it to suddenly wilt.

❤️ **TREAT IT** *If your plant has been outside in summer, drench the potting mix with an insecticide or biological control in the late summer or early fall to kill any grubs or repot in fresh potting mix. If they have eaten most of the roots, your plant will not recover.*

Look for grubs in the potting mix of your plant

Echeveria (pp.72–73)

APHIDS

Also known as greenflies, these can be green, black, gray, or orange. They gather on the tip of the stems and on flower buds, where they suck sap and secrete honeydew, which is then colonized by sooty mold. Aphids can also spread viruses.

TREAT IT *Rub them off by hand, dislodge with a spray of water, or spray with insecticide. Hanging a yellow sticky trap nearby can help.*

Nerve plant
leaf (pp.78–79)

SCALE INSECTS

These limpetlike insects look like brown lumps on the stems and the undersides of leaves. They also excrete a sticky sap, which can lead to sooty mold. If not controlled, your plant will be weakened and the leaves will turn yellow.

TREAT IT *Rub them off, or spray the affected areas with organic insecticide. (Don't spray the leaves of ferns, as they are very sensitive to chemicals.) You could also try a biological control.*

Scale insects cluster along the center of the leaves

Dwarf umbrella
tree leaf
(pp.120–121)

MEALYBUGS

These white, slow-moving insects coated in white fluff are found in clusters on stems, in leaf joints, and under leaves. They suck sap and excrete sticky honeydew, which then gets colonized by sooty mold. An infestation can lead to yellowing leaves, leaf fall, and wilting.

TREAT IT *Wipe off the insects with a damp cloth or cotton swab soaked with organic insecticide, or spray the whole plant with organic insecticide once a week. You could try a biological control. Mealybugs are hard to eradicate and it is often simpler to throw away severely infested plants.*

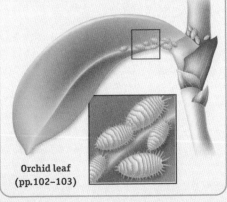

Orchid leaf
(pp.102–103)

PLANT DISEASES

Caring for your houseplants correctly is the best defense against disease, but stay vigilant! Here's how to spot and treat diseases that could attack your plant.

Gray mold spreading

African violet (pp.114–115)

The plant has collapsed

Cyclamen (pp.60–61)

Patches of white dust

Chinese money plant leaf (pp.110–111)

BOTRYTIS (OR GRAY MOLD)

Gray fluff can be found all over the plant, especially in cool, damp, or crowded conditions.

☀ **TREAT IT** *Water your plant from below to avoid splashing water on the leaves or crown. Remove any affected areas, along |with any moldy potting mix, and treat with organic fungicide. Water and mist less frequently. Improve ventilation.*

CROWN AND STEM ROT

The lower parts of the plant are dark, soft, and rotten, due to a fungal infection. It's usually caused by excess watering, splashing the base of the stems, or cool conditions.

☀ **TREAT IT** *You can try to save your plant by cutting out the affected area and treating it with organic fungicide. Avoid overwatering, and move the plant to a warmer, well-ventilated spot.*

POWDERY MILDEW

Patches of white dust will appear on the leaves and stems. It's more likely to occur where plants are crowded together and on overwatered plants. It's not fatal, but it can weaken your plant.

☀ **TREAT IT** *Remove the affected leaves, and treat your plant with organic fungicide. Space plants farther apart to improve airflow around them.*

Corky growths

Radiator plant leaf

OEDEMA

Look for corky growths on the underside of leaves. Oedema is caused by waterlogging, high humidity, and low light.

❤ **TREAT IT** *Water your plant less, reduce the humidity in the room, and move it to a brighter spot.*

Sooty mold

Dwarf umbrella tree leaf (pp.120–121)

SOOTY MOLD

This black fungus grows on the sticky waste of aphids, whiteflies, scale insects, and mealybugs. It blocks light and the plant's pores.

❤ **TREAT IT** *Sponge off the mold with a clean, damp cloth and treat the insect infestation (see Plant pests, pp.24–27).*

Mottled yellow markings

Wax flower leaf (pp.88–89)

VIRUSES

Signs include mottled, yellow foliage, distorted growth, and white streaks on the flowers.

❤ **TREAT IT** *A virus would have been transmitted by insects or was already present on the plant when it was bought. There is nothing you can do to save it.*

Leaf spot

Fiddle-leaf fig leaf (pp.76–77)

LEAF SPOT

Brown or black spots on the foliage are often surrounded by a yellow halo. Leaf spots can merge and kill an entire leaf. Caused by bacteria or fungi, they are more likely in damp or overcrowded conditions, or if water has been splashed on the leaves.

❤ **TREAT IT** *Remove any affected leaves and treat your plant with organic fungicide. Reduce humidity and space plants more widely.*

ROOT ROT

Caused by overwatering, root rot is a fungal infection of the roots that will lead to yellow, wilting leaves that turn brown, followed by the collapse of your plant. Affected roots will be soft and dark.

❤ **TREAT IT** *Remove the potting mix to check the roots. You can try to save it by trimming off any affected roots with a knife, leaving any healthy, white roots. Then cut the plant back to allow for the root reduction, treat with an organic fungicide, and repot in fresh potting mix and a disinfected pot.*

Soft, rotten areas

Prickly pear cactus (pp.98–99)

THE HOUSE-PLANTS

HOW TO TREASURE YOUR HOUSEPLANT
AND DEAL WITH ANY PROBLEMS

URN PLANT
Aechmea fasciata

Urn plants are exotic-looking bromeliads that have long-lasting flowers. The rosette of leaves forms a central "vase" that holds water.

HOW NOT TO KILL IT

LOCATION
Place the plant in a warm room that is 55–81°F (13–27°C). Good air circulation is important, so open a window on occasion.

LIGHT
Provide bright light, away from direct sun, which will burn the leaves.

WATERING + FEEDING
Water the central vase, ensuring the water is always 1in (2–3cm) deep. Use distilled, filtered, or rainwater. Empty and refill the vase every 2–3 weeks to prevent the water from stagnating. Water the potting mix in summer if the top 1in (2–3cm) is dry. Allow to drain after.

CARE
Provide high humidity if the room is warm—place it on a pebble-filled tray of water and mist the leaves 1–2 times a week.

BUG ALERT!
(see pp.24–27)
Prone to **mealybugs** and **scale insects** on the foliage.

BROWN, SOGGY LEAVES OR WILTING LEAVES?

This could be crown or root rot, caused by overwatering or poor drainage.

SAVE IT *Check for crown and root rot. Try trimming off the affected areas, treating with fungicide, and repotting in fresh potting mix. For more information, see Plant diseases (pp.28–29).*

← *Brown leaf*

FLOWER OR PLANT DYING BACK?

This is normal.

SAVE IT *Cut away the flower, as close to the foliage as you can, using a sharp knife. Urn plants only flower once, but if you continue to care for your plant, it will produce "pups" (new plants at its base). When they are a third the size of the main plant, cut them away carefully and pot them individually.*

PALE LEAVES?

The air is too dry or the plant is in direct sunlight.

☀♥ **SAVE IT** *Move your plant to a shadier spot and mist the leaves regularly.*

BROWN LEAF TIPS

This may be due to hot, dry air, or under- or overwatering. It can also be caused by hard tap water.

☀♥ **SAVE IT** *Add more water to the central vase and water the potting mix lightly. Mist the leaves more often. If you think hard water is the problem, switch to distilled, filtered, or rainwater.*

Aechmea fasciata

Height & spread: up to 20in (50cm)

SHARE THE CARE

FLAMING SWORD
Vriesea splendens
With its unusual, swordlike flower spike, this plant needs the same care as an urn plant.

GUZMANIA
Guzmania lingulata
This is another popular bromeliad with similar needs. It is known for its pineapplelike flower.

LIPSTICK PLANT
Aeschynanthus pulcher

This plant takes its name from the bright red flowers that emerge from their deep red cases in summer, just like lipsticks. Perfect for a hanging basket.

HOW NOT TO KILL IT

LOCATION
Place in a warm spot that stays between 64–81°F (18–27°C) year-round.

LIGHT
This plant likes it bright but out of direct sunlight.

WATERING + FEEDING
When the top layer of potting mix dries out, water with lukewarm rainwater or distilled water from spring to fall. Reduce watering in winter. Feed once a month in spring and summer.

CARE
Cut back any leggy shoots and repot in spring if very root-bound.

GRAY FLUFF ON THE LEAVES?
This could be a mold called botrytis.

SAVE IT *Remove any affected areas and treat with an organic fungicide. For more information, see Plant diseases (pp.28–29).*

NO FLOWERS?
The plant may not be getting enough light or nutrients.

SAVE IT *Try moving it to a brighter spot and/or feeding with a balanced fertilizer through spring and summer.*

LEAVES TURNING YELLOW OR PINKISH?
This means the plant is getting too much light.

SAVE IT *Try moving your plant to a slightly dimmer spot—keep it bright but out of direct sunlight.*

BUG ALERT!
(see pp.24–27)

Watch out for **aphids** and **mealybugs**.

SPOTS ON LEAVES?

Looks like the disease leaf spot, caused by a bacteria or fungus on the leaves.

💓 **SAVE IT** *Remove any affected leaves and treat with an organic fungicide (see Plant diseases, pp.28–29). Avoid splashing the leaves when watering to stop the disease from spreading.*

SHARE THE CARE

FISHBONE CACTUS
Disocactus anguliger

A tropical cactus with unusual wavy stems like the bones of a fish. Stunning white flowers appear for a day or two. Plant in cactus potting mix with additional grit, and keep between 52–57°F (11–14°C) in winter to encourage flowering.

Aeschynanthus pulcher

Height: up to 8in (20cm)

Spread: up to 28in (70cm)

ELEPHANT'S EAR
Alocasia x *amazonica*

Elephant's ears like hot, steamy conditions and have impressive, veined, dark green leaves.

HOW NOT TO KILL IT

LOCATION
Keep the plant at a temperature of 65–70°F (18–21°C) all year round. Avoid placing it near heat registers, air conditioning vents, and cold drafts.

LIGHT
Keep the plant out of direct sun in summer—bright, indirect light is best. In winter, move it to a brighter spot.

WATERING + FEEDING
Keep the potting mix moist (but not soggy) by watering lightly every few days. Use distilled, filtered, or rainwater that is lukewarm. Feed once a month during spring and summer. Water more sparingly in winter.

CARE
Alocasias love high humidity, so set the plant on a pebble-filled tray of water and mist the leaves frequently. Ensure that the pot has good drainage. Repot in spring, but only if the roots are significantly outgrowing the pot.

BROWN PATCHES ON THE LEAVES?

This is sunburn.

☀ **SAVE IT** *Move your plant to a more shaded spot, out of direct sunlight.*

Brown patches

PLANT DYING BACK?

If it is winter, your plant is probably going dormant, especially if temperatures fall below 60°F (15°C). If it isn't winter, it's not happy with its conditions.

☀ **SAVE IT** *If dormant, your plant should resprout in spring—continue to care for it as normal. Otherwise, check location, light, and watering regimen (see left).*

BUG ALERT!
(see pp.24–27)

Prone to **mealybugs, scale insects**, and **spider mites** on the foliage.

BROWN, CRISPY LEAVES?

Either the air is too hot and dry, or chemicals in hard tap water are causing issues.

SAVE IT *Move to a cooler, more humid location. Watering with distilled, filtered, or rainwater may help.*

Brown, crispy leaf

PLANT WILTING?

This could be due to under- or overwatering. Overwatering can lead to root rot.

SAVE IT *Check the potting mix and adjust your watering regimen if it is too dry or wet. If the problem persists, check for root rot. Remove any affected areas, treat with organic fungicide, and repot in new potting mix. For more information, see Plant diseases (pp.28–29).*

Alocasia x amazonica

Height & spread: up to 5ft (1.5m)

ALOE VERA
Aloe vera

This easy-to-grow succulent has spiky, fleshy leaves. The sap is used to soothe burns and skin irritations.

HOW NOT TO KILL IT

LOCATION
Keep it in a room that is 50–75°F (10–24°C). Happy, mature plants will produce yellow flowers.

LIGHT
Place in a bright spot (e.g. a south-facing window). It will cope with some direct sun, but acclimate it gradually.

WATERING + FEEDING
In spring and summer, water when the top 1in (2–3cm) of potting mix has dried out—this may be once a week, depending on its position. In winter, water very sparingly. Feed once in spring and once in summer.

CARE
Aloes like well-drained potting mix, so add potting sand or perlite when planting, or use cactus mix. A layer of sand on the top will keep the neck dry and prevent rot. Only repot if the plant has outgrown its pot. The plant will produce baby "offsets"—these can be left on the plant, or cut off at the base with their roots and planted individually.

SHRUNKEN, WRINKLED LEAVES?

Your plant needs watering or may have root rot due to overwatering.

SAVE IT *Water lightly and mist the leaves. Repeat for the next two days—the leaves should plump up. Don't let your plant sit in very wet potting mix.*

LEAVES TURNING BROWN, RED, OR REDDISH BROWN?

Your plant could be getting too much sun in the middle of the day during summer, or it may be overwatered. The roots may also be damaged.

SAVE IT *Move your plant to a bright spot with less direct sunlight. Reduce watering. If it doesn't recover, check the roots.*

— *Reddish brown leaf*

PALE OR YELLOWING LEAVES?

If your whole plant is pale or yellowing, it has been overwatered, or it isn't getting enough light.

♥ **SAVE IT** *Ensure that you are watering the plant correctly (see left). Move it to a brighter spot.*

DARK SPOTS? BROWN OR MUSHY LEAVES?

This is most likely due to overwatering.

♥ **SAVE IT** *Do not water until the potting mix has dried out. Ensure that the pot has drainage holes. Avoid spilling water on the foliage, as it will gather at the base and cause rot.*

Dark spots

Aloe vera
Height & spread: up to 3ft (1m)

SHARE THE CARE

AGAVE
Agave
Ideal for a sunny windowsill, this succulent needs the same care as an aloe. Some varieties have very sharp spines.

HAWORTHIA
Haworthia
Another spiky succulent with the same care needs. In direct sun, the leaves may turn red.

ANTHURIUM
Anthurium

Also called flamingo flower, this easy-to-grow houseplant has wavy, exotic, brightly colored flowers (spathes) that can last for weeks.

HOW NOT TO KILL IT

LOCATION
An anthurium is a tropical plant, so it needs warmth and humidity. Place the plant in a warm room (60–68°F/15–20°C) and away from drafts.

LIGHT
Position it in bright light, but out of direct sun, about 3ft (1m) or so away from a sunny window.

WATERING + FEEDING
Water moderately from spring to fall, whenever the soil surface feels dry. After watering, the potting mix should feel moist, but not soggy. Water less in winter. Feed monthly in spring and summer.

CARE
To provide humidity, mist the leaves regularly (avoiding the flowers) or set the plant on a pebble-filled tray of water. Clean the leaves frequently with a damp sponge, and gently pull off spent flowers. Repot in spring into a slightly larger pot.

BUG ALERT!
(see pp.24–27)

Prone to **mealybugs** and **red spider mites** on the foliage.

Brown leaf tips

LEAF TIPS TURNING BROWN?

The air in the room is too hot and dry, your plant is being under- or overwatered, or it is sitting in a drafty spot.

SAVE IT *Move your plant away from the heat source if necessary and check your watering regime.*

*Anthurium
andraeanum*

Height & spread:
up to 20in
(50cm)

LOTS OF LEAVES
BUT NO FLOWERS?

Your plant may not be getting enough
sunlight, it might be in too large a pot,
or it may be underfed.

❤ **SAVE IT** *Move it to a brighter
spot. Repot it in a smaller pot if there is
more than ½–¾in (1–2cm) between
the edge of the pot and the root ball.
Feed once a month to encourage
flowering (see left).*

YELLOWING LEAVES?

An occasional yellow leaf is likely aging.
If widespread, it could be too much or
too little watering, lack of feeding, cold
drafts, or the plant is root-bound.

❤ **SAVE IT** *Adjust the feeding and
watering regime—but don't let it sit in
water—and consider moving or repotting.*

FOXTAIL FERN
Asparagus densiflorus 'Myersii'

While it may look delicate, the foxtail "fern" is an easy-to-grow plant that will tolerate a little drought and dry air, unlike a true fern.

HOW NOT TO KILL IT

LOCATION
Keep this plant in a room that stays between 55–75°F (13–24°C) and is away from drafts to keep it looking its best.

LIGHT
Position in light shade or filtered sun.

WATERING + FEEDING
Keep the potting mix moist from spring to summer, but let the top layer of potting mix dry out between waterings in winter. Feed once a month with a half-strength fertilizer from spring to fall.

CARE
Cut away any leggy or brown fronds at the base. Repot when root-bound into a pot one size up.

BUG ALERT!
(see pp.24–27)

Check for **red spider mites**, **mealybugs**, and **scale** among the fronds.

Asparagus densiflorus 'Myersii'
Height and spread: up to 2ft (60cm)

LEAF EDGES TURNING BROWN?

Either the plant is sitting in direct sunlight or the potting mix is drying out in the warmer months.

SAVE IT *Move the plant to a shadier spot and make sure to keep the potting mix moist in spring and summer.*

Faded leaf

BASE OF PLANT BROWN OR MUSHY?

The mushy parts of the plant are rotting. This is a sign of crown or stem rot.

SAVE IT *Remove any rotten parts and make sure to water carefully around the sides of the plant so that water does not collect in the crown. Ensure the pot has good drainage.*

LEAVES TURNING YELLOW?

Older leaves will turn yellow on a healthy plant and can be cut away. If lots of them turn yellow, check whether the plant is sitting in full sun or if the temperature is too high. This can also be a symptom of root rot.

SAVE IT *Move it away from heat sources and out of direct sunlight. Check that the pot is draining well and that the roots are healthy.*

Widespread yellowing

SHARE THE CARE

ASPARAGUS FERN
Asparagus setaceus
It has similar care needs, but this plant likes higher humidity than its cousin and can tolerate less light.

EMERALD FERN
Asparagus densiflorus
Sprengeri Group
A selection of the same species as the Foxtail, but with more feathery foliage. It needs cooler temperatures of 45–70°F (7–21°C).

POLKA-DOT BEGONIA
Begonia maculata

A Brazilian showstopper with large white-spotted leaves and tumbling cream flowers in summer. Stake stems to keep them upright.

· ·

HOW NOT TO KILL IT

LOCATION
Ideally, keep the plant at around 64–70°F (18–21°C) all year round, but don't let it get any hotter. They can survive at 55°F (13°C) in winter, but no colder.

LIGHT
Place it in good but indirect light. Avoid direct sun, which can burn the leaves.

WATERING + FEEDING
Water so the potting mix is moist, but allow it to dry out a little in between waterings during summer. It is best watered from below to stop water from accumulating at the base of the stems (see Water it, pp.18–19). Keep just moist in winter. Apply a high-nitrogen fertilizer every two weeks from spring to fall.

CARE
Cut back leggy stems and repot if necessary in spring. Turn the pot regularly to ensure the plant grows evenly. Make sure it has good ventilation.

> **BUG ALERT!**
> (see pp.24–27)
> Prone to **aphids**, **red spider mites**, **whitefly**, and **thrips**.

Begonia maculata
Height: up to 36in (90cm)
Spread: up to 18in (45cm)

YELLOWING LEAVES?

These could be due to too much or too little water or not enough light.

💗 **SAVE IT** *Check your plant's care regime and position (see left).*

GRAY FLUFF ON PARTS OF THE PLANT?

This is gray mold (botrytis), due to cool, damp, crowded conditions or water splashing onto the leaves.

💗 **SAVE IT** *Move the plant away from other begonias to stop the infection from spreading and improve ventilation. Remove any affected areas and treat with organic fungicide (see Plant diseases, pp.28–29).*

WHITE POWDER ON THE LEAVES?

This is powdery mildew, often due to drought or poor air circulation.

💗 **SAVE IT** *Remove the affected leaves and treat with organic fungicide. For more information, see Plant diseases (pp.28–29).*

LOSING LEAVES?

Your plant may be overwatered or too hot. If it's getting leggy, too, it doesn't have enough light.

💗 **SAVE IT** *Move it to a brighter spot, out of direct sunlight. Check the temperature and your watering regime (see left).*

SHARE THE CARE

ELIATOR HYBRIDS
Begonia **Eliator Group**
These have small, pretty flowers in a range of colors. Deadhead regularly to prolong flowering.

PAINTED-LEAF BEGONIA
Begonia rex
There are many varieties of painted-leaf begonias that have beautiful foliage in shades of crimson, silver, purple, green, and red. Place in filtered sun for the best colors.

TOP 5 PLANTS FOR
YOUR DESK

Greening up your workspace is said to boost productivity and reduce stress, with scientific studies revealing that certain plants can remove toxins from the air. A good desk plant is compact, and not too fussy about light levels.

Lucky bamboo
Dracaena sanderiana

We can't guarantee that this plant will get you a raise or a promotion, but it will bring cheer to your working day. Grow it in potting mix or even just in a glass of distilled, filtered, or rainwater.

See Lucky bamboo, pp.70–71.

Blushing bromeliad
Neoregelia carolinae f. tricolor

This attractive plant is grown for its foliage, which blushes pink just before it flowers. Keep its central "vase" topped off with bottled water.

See Blushing bromeliad, p.49.

African spear

Sansevieria cylindrica

This striking foliage plant is related to the spiky snake plant, and has cylindrical leaves. It's a low-maintenance plant that doesn't need much watering—so it can tolerate a bit of neglect if you go away.

See African spear, p.117.

Watermelon peperomia

Peperomia argyreia

An easy-to-care-for tropical beauty, this species of peperomia has dark green, patterned leaves that resemble the skin of watermelon.

See Watermelon peperomia, pp.100–101.

Dracaena marginata

Dracaena marginata

This easygoing plant is a good air purifier, and doesn't mind erratic watering. It can get quite tall, but it doesn't take up much room as it has a very thin trunk. Keep it in a lightly shaded spot.

See Dracaena marginata, pp.68–69.

QUEEN'S TEARS
Billbergia nutans

This is one of the easiest bromeliads to grow. Try displaying queen's tears in a hanging planter.

BUG ALERT!
(see pp.24–27)

Prone to **mealybugs** and **scale insects** on the foliage.

HOW NOT TO KILL IT

LOCATION
Keep the plant in a room that is 41–75°F (5–24°C). It will only flower if at the upper end of this range.

LIGHT
Place in bright but indirect light.

WATERING + FEEDING
Water the "vase" (the center of the rosette of leaves) with distilled, filtered, or rainwater, ensuring that the water is always 1in (2–3cm) deep. Empty and refill the vase every 2–3 weeks to prevent the water from stagnating. Keep the potting mix just moist. Feed once a month in spring and summer by adding half-strength liquid fertilizer to the central vase.

CARE
Place the plant on a pebble-filled tray of water for humidity. It will flower at around 3 years old. Gently pull faded flowers away. Repot after flowering in spring. It will produce "pups" (new plants at the base), dying slowly in the process. Repot pups when they are one-third the size of the parent.

LEAF TIPS TURNING YELLOW?
Your plant has probably outgrown its container.

☀ **SAVE IT** *Repot your plant in spring, after it has flowered.*

BROWN LEAF TIPS?

This could be due to dry air or watering with hard water.

💜 **SAVE IT** *Mist the leaves regularly, if warm. Switch to distilled, filtered, or rainwater.*

DRIPPING FLOWERS?

This is nectar, which drips from the flowers when they are moved or touched—hence Billbergia's common name, queen's tears.

💜 **SAVE IT** *Do nothing!*

Billbergia nutans

Height & spread: up to 20in (50cm)

NO FLOWERS?

Your plant won't flower until it's around 3 years old. If you have a mature plant, the temperature may be too low, or it may be in too dark a spot.

💜 **SAVE IT** *Move it to a warmer spot in a bright position. Avoid placing it in direct sunlight.*

SHARE THE CARE

PINK QUILL
Tillandsia cyanea
This bromeliad has similar care needs as queen's tears but prefers a warmer room (57–77°F/14–25°C).

BLUSHING BROMELIAD
Neoregelia carolinae f. tricolor
Provide the same care as for pink quill. The central vase turns red ("blushes") before it flowers.

PEACOCK PLANT
Calathea

Most peacock plants are grown for their beautifully patterned leaves. Calathea leaves often have burgundy red undersides.

. . . .

HOW NOT TO KILL IT

 LOCATION
It is a rainforest plant, so keep it in a warm room (60–68°F/16–20°C), but away from a heat source. Avoid rooms with sudden temperature fluctuations.

 LIGHT
Put it in partial shade or bright light. Keep it away from direct sun.

WATERING + FEEDING
From spring to fall, keep the potting mix moist (but not wet) at all times. Use distilled, filtered, or rainwater as these plants are sensitive to chemicals added to tap water. Make sure the pot drains well. Water more sparingly in winter. Feed once in spring, summer, and fall.

 CARE
To help maintain humidity, keep your plant away from heat sources; grouping with other plants can also improve humidity. Wipe the leaves occasionally to keep them free of dust. Repot in spring.

> **BUG ALERT!**
> (see pp.24–27)
>
> Prone to **spider mites** on the foliage.

Calathea roseopicta
Height: up to 9½in (24cm)
Spread: up to 6in (15cm)

DROOPY LEAVES?

You could be overwatering or underwatering. Alternatively, your plant may be too cold or exposed to drafts.

❤ **SAVE IT** *The potting mix should be moist, but not wet. Water sparingly in winter. Try moving your plant to a warmer, sheltered spot.*

LEAVES CURLING AT THE EDGES?

You are probably underwatering your plant.

❤ **SAVE IT** *Check your watering regime (see left).*

PRAYER PLANT
Maranta
A prayer plant has the same needs as a peacock plant. The leaves fold at night like human hands in prayer.

Brown leaf edge

LEAF TIPS OR EDGES BROWN?

The air is probably too hot and dry, you may have overfed your plant, or it may be due to watering with hard water.

❤ **SAVE IT** *Move away from the heat source. Group with other plants to increase humidity. Switch to watering with distilled, filtered, or rainwater.*

FADED OR SCORCHED LEAVES?

Your plant has probably been in direct sunlight.

❤ **SAVE IT** *Move it to a shadier place.*

Faded leaf

STROMANTHE
Stromanthe
A stromanthe likes more humidity than a peacock plant. Keep it above 65°F (18°C) and don't water it with cold or hard water.

CURLY SPIDER PLANT
Chlorophytum comosum 'Bonnie'

Just as easy to care for as its more common cousin, the curly spider plant has striped leaves that twist and curl in, giving it a compact shape.

HOW NOT TO KILL IT

 LOCATION
Keep this plant between 45–75°F (7–24°C).

 LIGHT
Place it out of direct sun in a bright room.

 WATERING + FEEDING
Keep the potting mix moist during the summer months, but not wet. Reduce in winter. Feed monthly from spring to summer.

CARE
Repot whenever root-bound. The baby plants or plantlets that grow on long stems can be cut off and grown as new plants. Place them in potting mix if they have roots and in water if they have none until roots appear.

BUG ALERT! (see pp.24–27)	Check under the leaves for **red spider mites** and **scale insects**.

THE LEAVES ARE PALE?
Intense sunlight, low light, underwatering, and low temperatures can all cause the leaves to turn pale.

SAVE IT *Water attentively, remove it from direct sun, and check temperatures. Make sure it is getting enough light in winter.*

LEAVES STREAKED WITH BROWN IN THE WINTER?
This happens when plants are overwatered in winter.

SAVE IT *You can remove any brown leaves at the base. Reduce watering in the winter so that the potting mix is just moist.*

SLOW OR NO GROWTH?
Incorrect levels of light, water, or nutrients can cause this, as well as pot-bound roots.

SAVE IT *Make sure it is getting enough light, water, and feed in spring and summer. Repot if roots are crowded.*

LEAF TIPS ARE BROWN?

Hot and dry air can cause this, as well as underwatering and underfeeding.

☀️❤️ **SAVE IT** *Remove any brown parts, move the plant away from heat sources, or move to a room with higher humidity. Feed and water it regularly from spring to summer.*

Chlorophytum comosum 'Bonnie'

Height: up to 8in (20cm)

Spread: up to 12in (30cm)

SHARE THE CARE

POTHOS
Epipremnum

This plant has similar needs to a spider plant and will climb up a moss pole or trail from a pot.

GRAPE IVY
Cissus rhombifolia

Another easy-to-care-for houseplant. Grape ivy has glossy, lobed, dark green leaves and will trail gracefully from a hanging basket or up a trellis to cover a wall.

CLIVIA
Clivia miniata

Clivias are native to South Africa
and produce a beautiful, single, red, orange,
or yellow flower in early spring.

HOW NOT TO KILL IT

LOCATION
From spring to late fall, keep the
plant in a heated room. In winter, rest it for
3 months in a room that will remain around
50°F (10°C)—this will help initiate growth of
a flower bud. Then return it to its spring-to-
fall position.

LIGHT
Provide bright, but indirect light.

WATERING + FEEDING
From spring to late fall, keep the
potting mix moist. Reduce watering in
winter so that the mix is almost dry. Feed
once a month from spring to fall, and not
at all during winter.

CARE
Wipe the leaves occasionally. Don't
move the pot when the plant is flowering
or in bud. After flowering, cut off the dead
flower spike at the base. The plant may
produce a second flower in late summer.
Clivias like to be snug, so repot the plant
after flowering only if the roots are bursting
out of the pot.

BLEACHED OR BROWN PATCHES ON THE LEAVES?

The leaves are sunburned.

SAVE IT *Move
your plant out of
direct sunlight.*

*Bleached patches
on the leaves*

BUG ALERT!
(see pp.24–27)

Prone to **mealybugs**
and **spider mites**
on the foliage.

BROWN LEAVES AT THE BASE OF YOUR PLANT?

This happens when the older leaves
are dying back.

SAVE IT *This is normal. Just
gently pull away any brown leaves.*

YELLOW LEAVES?

This could be due to underfeeding, or under- or overwatering.

☀ **SAVE IT** *Make sure you are using the correct watering and feeding regimen for the season (see left).*

Yellow ⎯ leaves

SHORT FLOWER SPIKE?
NO FLOWER IN SPRING?

This is most likely due to a lack of rest in winter, but it could be because the pot is too large, or because your plant was underwatered after being rested.

☀ **SAVE IT** *If it has been rested, make sure you keep the potting mix moist. Check that the pot is not too big—the root ball should only be 1in (2–3cm) away from the edge of the pot.*

Clivia miniata

Height: up to
18in (45cm)

Spread: up to
12in (30cm)

JADE PLANT
Crassula ovata

This low-maintenance, long-lasting succulent looks like a tiny tree and is said to bring good fortune. It can produce flowers in winter.

HOW NOT TO KILL IT

LOCATION
Position the plant on a sunny windowsill that is 50–75°F (18–24°C). It will tolerate periods at 50°F (10°C) in winter.

LIGHT
Provide bright, dappled sunlight.

WATERING + FEEDING
Water moderately; let the top 1in (2–3cm) of potting mix dry out between waterings. Water more sparingly in winter. Feed once in spring and then again in summer.

CARE
Pull off any old, shriveled leaves. In spring, lightly prune the plant to shape. Plant it in a weighty pot as it can become top-heavy and topple over.

DISCOLORED?
Purple or red leaves could mean lack of water or too much sun; yellow leaves may be overwatering.

SAVE IT *Check the plant's position and watering regime.*

DROPPING LEAVES?
Older leaves will shrivel and fall off naturally, but younger leaves may drop under environmental stress (such as being moved to bright sunlight suddenly, or over- or underwatering).

SAVE IT *Give water if the potting mix is very dry, or allow it to dry out if soggy. When repositioning, move your plant gradually toward the desired spot over a week, to allow it to acclimate.*

BUG ALERT!
(see pp.24–27)

Prone to **mealybugs** on the stems and leaves.

Dropped leaves

SHRIVELED LEAVES AND STEMS?

Your plant is short of water.

☀ **SAVE IT** *Give your plant a small amount of water daily over the course of a few days—the leaves should soon plump up again. Don't let it stand in soggy potting mix.*

Shriveled leaves

STRING OF PEARLS
Senecio rowleyanus
This eye-catching hanging plant has similar needs to a jade plant.

Crassula ovata

Height & spread: up to 3ft (1m)

LEGGY PLANT?

Your plant needs more sunlight.

☀ **SAVE IT** *Move it to a sunnier spot.*

HEARTS ON A STRING
Ceropegia woodii
This fleshy-leaved plant has similar needs and is great for a hanging planter.

NEVER-NEVER PLANT
Ctenanthe burle-marxii

This is also known as the fishbone prayer plant due to the patterning of its leaves—striped dark green with red undersides—and their quality of curling up at night like hands in prayer.

HOW NOT TO KILL IT

LOCATION
Native to the rainforest, this plant needs to be kept in a warm room (60–68°F/16–20°C) away from a heat source. Avoid rooms with sudden temperature fluctuations.

LIGHT
Place in bright light or partial shade. Keep out of direct sun.

WATERING + FEEDING
Keep the potting mix moist but not wet at all times from spring through fall. Let the top layer of potting mix dry out between waterings in winter, and make sure the pot has good drainage. Use distilled, filtered, or rainwater. Feed monthly from spring to fall with a balanced fertilizer.

CARE
Wipe leaves with a damp cloth to remove dust. Repot every two to three years or when root-bound. Keep your plant away from a heat source.

BUG ALERT!
(see pp.24–27)
Vulnerable to **mealybugs** and **red spider mites**.

LEAVES ROLLING UP?
Your plant needs more water or is overheating.

SAVE IT *Increase watering but ensure the pot drains well and the soil is not wet. Move the plant away from a heat source.*

LEAF TIPS OR EDGES BROWN?

You may be watering with hard water, overfeeding your plant, or the air in the room is too hot and dry.

❤️ **SAVE IT** *Move away from heat sources. Switch to distilled, filtered, or rainwater.*

SHARE THE CARE

CROTON
Codiaeum variegatum

A croton requires similar care to the never-never plant but likes humidity. Also needs to be protected from fluctuating temperatures.

Ctenanthe burle-marxii

Height: up to 24in (60cm)

Spread: up to 18in (45cm)

FADED OR SCORCHED LEAVES?

The plant has been in direct sunlight.

❤️ **SAVE IT** *Move it to a shadier place.*

CYCLAMEN
Cyclamen persicum

Cyclamen makes a charming indoor plant, adorned from fall to spring with bright flowers.

....

HOW NOT TO KILL IT

LOCATION
A cyclamen should flower for several months in a cool room, if bought in bud in fall (the start of the flowering season). It won't like high temperatures, but don't let it freeze either—keeping it at 50–60°F (10–15°C) is best.

LIGHT
Keep out of direct sunlight—a north-facing windowsill would be ideal.

WATERING + FEEDING
Keep the potting mix just moist, watering from below by setting the plant in a saucer of water for about 30 minutes (see Water it pp.18–19). This avoids getting the leaves and stems wet.

CARE
Remove spent flowers or dead leaves by giving them a sharp tug or snipping them off. Most plants are discarded after they flower, but it is possible to keep them going from year to year (see No more flowers?).

Yellowed leaf

YELLOW FOLIAGE?

Your plant is too warm, has been over- or underwatered, or exposed to direct sunlight. If it's spring, it may be dying back naturally.

💧 **SAVE IT** *Remove yellow leaves. Move it out of direct sunlight, and to a place around 60°F (15°C). Keep the potting mix just moist, watering from below (see Water it, pp.18–19).*

POOR FLOWERING?

Your plant will flower best in lower temperatures, as high temperatures will send it into early dormancy. If it's nearing the end of the season, your plant will stop flowering.

♥ **SAVE IT** *Check that your plant isn't in too warm a spot to flower, and make sure you are caring for it correctly (see left). Buy cyclamen in fall and look for plants with lots of buds. These will be the longest-flowering plants as the buds will open into new flowers as the older ones fade.*

SHARE THE CARE

INDOOR AZALEA
Rhododendron simsii
Care for an indoor azalea in the same way as a cyclamen, keeping the potting mix moist and watering it with soft water or rainwater, as it doesn't like lime. Needs a cool spot to flower well.

PLANT HAS COLLAPSED?

This is probably because your plant is getting too much **or too little** water, and may be due to crown rot.

♥ **SAVE IT** *Look for crown rot at the base of the stems; remove affected areas. For more information, see Plant diseases (pp.28–29). Crown rot is likely to kill your plant.*

Crown rot

Cyclamen persicum
Height: up to 8in (20cm)
Spread: up to 6in (15cm)

NO MORE FLOWERS?

Cyclamen dies back and goes dormant over summer.

☀ **SAVE IT** *Stop watering your plant when it stops flowering and the leaves turn yellow and wither in spring. Place your plant outside in a dry, shaded place over summer, keeping the potting mix just moist. If you live in a wet area, put the pot on its side so that any rainwater drains out. In fall, bring the plant back indoors and, when you see regrowth, start watering again.*

DIEFFENBACHIA
Dieffenbachia seguine

The lush green and cream leaves of dieffenbachia will brighten a gloomy corner, but take care, as the leaf sap contains calcium oxalate, which can cause irritation and swelling.

HOW NOT TO KILL IT

 LOCATION
Keep it in a warm room that is 60–75°F (16–24°C). Dieffenbachias don't like cold drafts or dry air.

 LIGHT
Place it in a partially shaded location in summer. Move it to a brighter spot in winter.

 WATERING + FEEDING
From spring to fall, water whenever the top 1in (2–3cm) of potting mix is dry. Water sparingly in winter. Feed once a month.

CARE
Provide humidity by misting the leaves regularly and placing the plant on a pebble-filled tray of water. Wipe the leaves once a month. Repot in spring.

BUG ALERT!
(see pp.24–27) | Prone to **mealybugs** on the foliage.

YELLOWING LOWER LEAVES?

Low temperatures or drafts are probably the reason.

☀ **SAVE IT** *Move it to a warmer room, somewhere free of drafts.*

PALE LEAVES?

Too much bright light or direct sun will make the leaves look bleached and washed out.

☀ **SAVE IT** *Move your plant to a shadier spot.*

LEAVES DROPPING?

The room may be too cold or drafty for your plant.

💗 **SAVE IT** *Check for drafts and then place your plant in a warmer location.*

BROWN EDGES ON THE LEAVES?

The potting mix may be too dry, or either dry or cold air may be the cause. Another possibility is that your plant has been overfed.

💗 **SAVE IT** *Water until the potting mix feels moist, but not soggy, and allow only the top 1in (2–3cm) of mix to dry out between waterings. Increase the humidity around your plant, move it to a warmer spot, and check your feeding regimen (see left).*

Dieffenbachia seguine

Height & spread: up to 24in (60cm)

SHARE THE CARE

ARROWHEAD PLANT
Syngonium podophyllum
Care for as you would a spider plant. It will climb or trail, and looks great in a hanging planter.

SHAMROCK PLANT
Oxalis triangularis
This pretty plant has similar care requirements. It is a bulb, so dies back in winter.

VENUS FLYTRAP
Dionaea muscipula

This fascinating, carnivorous plant has traps
that snap shut when an insect lands on them.
The captured insect is then slowly digested.

HOW NOT TO KILL IT

 LOCATION
Place the plant on a south-facing
windowsill in a moderately warm room
(45–70°F/7–21°C). In winter, rest it in
an unheated room (45°F/7°C).

 LIGHT
Provide bright sunlight, some direct.

WATERING + FEEDING
Keep the potting mix moist in the
growing season (set it in a saucer of water),
and just moist during its resting period.
Use distilled, filtered, or rainwater. Do not
use fertilizer as the plant gets its nutrients
from the insects it catches. If there are no
insects indoors, place it outside for a few
days at a time during summer to catch prey.

CARE
Plant it in a very low-nutrient,
1:1 mix of peat moss and perlite. Cut off
the dead traps with scissors. The plant
may flower in summer. It's best to cut
off the flowers as these will weaken the
plant. Repot if necessary in early spring.

Green, floppy lobes

RED LOBES TURNING GREEN AND FLOPPY?

This is a sign that your plant isn't happy
with your watering regimen or humidity.
The plant may die suddenly if this is not
remedied quickly.

SAVE IT *Increase
humidity by misting the
leaves. Check your watering
regimen (see left).*

BLACKENED TRAPS?

Traps often die
off in fall and
winter as the plant
goes dormant.

SAVE IT *This is
normal. When the plant
comes back into growth
after the winter, it will
produce new traps.*

YELLOW, BROWN, OR BLACK TRAPS?

This can happen if your plant is moved from a shady spot to a very sunny one too quickly.

☀ **SAVE IT** *Acclimate your plant to brighter spots gradually over the course of a week.*

← *Burned leaves*

TRAP NOT CLOSING?

This is likely to be the result of curious fingers poking at your plant too many times.

❤ **SAVE IT** *Each trap will only close four or five times in its lifetime, so resist "teasing" your plant.*

SHARE THE CARE

PITCHER PLANT
Sarracenia
This plant attracts insects that fall into it and drown. It has the same needs as a Venus flytrap.

BUG ALERT!
(see pp.24–27)

Prone to **aphids** and **spider mites**.

Dionaea muscipula

Height: up to 18in (45cm)

Spread: up to 6in (15cm)

MONKEY CUPS
Nepenthes
Insects are trapped in the brightly colored pitchers of this plant. Care for it as you would a venus flytrap.

TOP 5 PLANTS FOR
SUNNY SPOTS

The sun's rays can scorch the foliage of many houseplants, but some plants, including desert cacti and succulents, love sunshine. Acclimate them gradually and shade plants from very strong midday sun in summer. They look great grouped together; here are five to try.

Echeveria
Echeveria

This rosette-forming succulent can cope with some direct sunlight. An Echeveria will produce pretty, yellow, orange, or pink, bell-shaped flowers.

See Echeveria, pp.72–73.

Bunny ears cactus
Opuntia microdasys

Cacti come in a fascinating range of shapes and sizes. This cactus is native to the deserts of Mexico and naturalized in parts of East Africa—it is therefore no surprise it loves bright light!

See Bunny ears cactus, pp.98–99.

Jade plant
Crassula ovata

This plant needs lots of bright light, and can tolerate some direct sunlight. It is often quite small when bought, so is perfect for a sunny windowsill. It will last many years and may produce small flowers each winter.

See Jade plant, pp.56–57.

Aloe vera
Aloe vera

This spiky succulent enjoys being in a very bright location, and can even cope with some direct sunlight. A mature aloe will produce offsets (new baby plants) at its base.

See Aloe vera, pp.38–39.

Venus flytrap
Dionaea muscipula

This fun plant needs lots of bright light and some direct sunlight. When an insect lands on the hinged leaves, they snap shut, trapping the prey inside.

See Venus flytrap, pp.64–65.

DRACAENA COMPACTA
Dracaena fragrans

Grown for their palmlike leaves, dracaena are easy-going indoor shrubs that don't mind erratic watering.

HOW NOT TO KILL IT

 LOCATION
Place the plant close to an east- or west-facing window in a room that is 55–70°F (13–21°C).

 LIGHT
Keep it out of direct sunlight.

 WATERING + FEEDING
From spring to fall, water freely when the top 1in (2–3cm) of the potting mix has become dry. In winter, keep the mix just moist. Feed monthly from spring to fall, but not during winter. They can survive irregular watering to a certain extent.

CARE
Wipe the leaves occasionally, pulling away any that are dead. The plant needs humidity, so place it on a pebble-filled tray of water and mist a few times a week.

BUG ALERT!
(see pp.24–27)

Look for **mealybugs** and **scale insects** on the foliage.

WILTING LEAVES?

You may be watering your plant too little or too much. It may also have root rot.

SAVE IT *Make sure you are watering correctly (see left). Check that the pot has good drainage. If the problem persists, check for root rot and remove any affected areas. For more information, see Plant diseases (pp.28–29).*

BROWN TIPS ON THE LEAVES?

Brown edges could indicate too much fertilizer or a watering issue. Dracaenas can also be sensitive to the chemicals in tap water.

❤ **SAVE IT** *Check your watering regime and use distilled, filtered, or rainwater. for the season (see left).*

YELLOWING LEAVES AT THE BASE?

Each leaf will naturally turn yellow and fall off after a couple of years.

❤ **SAVE IT** *Don't worry! Just gently pull away the yellowed leaves to remove them.*

Yellowing leaf →

Dracaena fragrans

Height: up to 5ft (1.5m)

Spread: up to 30in (75cm)

SHARE THE CARE

DRACAENA MARGINATA
Dracaena marginata
The dracaena marginata has the same care requirements. It's narrow, so it's good if you're short on space.

SONG OF INDIA
Dracaena reflexa
Another dracaena with the same needs. Its lush, palm-like leaves are arranged in a spiral around the main stem.

LUCKY BAMBOO
Dracaena sanderiana

Popularly used in feng shui, this plant is often sold with twisted stems. It can be grown in potting mix or water.

HOW NOT TO KILL IT

LOCATION
Keep the plant at 60–75°F (16–24°C), and no colder than 50°F (10°C) in winter. Avoid drafty spots or places with large temperature fluctuations.

LIGHT
Place it in a bright spot, away from direct sunlight.

WATERING + FEEDING
Use distilled, filtered, or rainwater as the plant is sensitive to the chemicals in tap water. If growing in potting mix, water when the mix has become slightly dry to the touch. Reduce watering in winter. Feed once in spring and once in summer. Plants growing in water should be given a weak feeding every couple of months.

CARE
If the plant is being grown in potting mix, repot it every 2 years. If growing in water, the water needs a depth of at least 2in (5cm)—make sure the roots are covered. Refresh with lukewarm water every week.

BROWN LEAF TIPS?

In plants growing in potting mix or water, this may be due to chemicals in tap water or because the room is too dry.

SAVE IT *Use distilled, filtered, or rainwater. If you think low humidity may be to blame, mist the leaves every couple of days.*

ALGAE IN THE WATER?

This will only affect plants grown in water, and is caused by chemicals in tap water, or by too much light.

SAVE IT *Clean the container and pebbles. You might want to switch to an opaque container, and fill it with distilled, filtered, or rainwater. Move your plant away from direct sunlight.*

LEAVES STRETCHING OR PALE GREEN?

Your plant is not getting enough light.

❤️ **SAVE IT** *Move to a brighter spot.*

BUG ALERT!
(see pp.24–27)

Prone to **mealybugs** and **red spider mites** on foliage.

YELLOW LEAVES?

Your plant may have been exposed to temperature changes or too much sun, or it may have been overfed or underwatered.

❤️ **SAVE IT** *Move your plant out of direct sun and ensure it is a consistent temperature. Check your watering regimen and reduce feeding if necessary.*

YELLOW STEMS?

This is due to a lack of water, stagnant water, overfeeding, temperature fluctuations, or too much or too little light. The stems will not recover.

❤️ **SAVE IT** *Remove the affected stems right away. Check your watering and feeding regimen. If growing in water, replace the water with fresh distilled, filtered, or rainwater.*

Yellow stem

Dracaena sanderiana

Height: up to 3ft (90cm)

Spread: up to 4in (10cm)

ECHEVERIA
Echeveria

There are many varieties of this succulent, all producing tiny flowers on tall stems.

HOW NOT TO KILL IT

 LOCATION
Keep the plant at 50–75°F (10–24°C). It can tolerate lower temperatures if the potting mix isn't wet.

 LIGHT
Provide lots of bright light. The plant can take some direct sunlight, as long as it is acclimated gradually.

 WATERING + FEEDING
From spring to fall, water when the top 1in (2–3cm) of potting mix is dry. Water sparingly in winter. Feed once a month in spring and summer.

CARE
Top the potting mix with a layer of gravel—this will keep the neck of the plant dry and will show off the whole plant nicely. Don't choose too large a pot as it will do better if a little cramped. Add some horticultural sand to the mix when planting to improve drainage. Baby plants need more care than large, established ones. Plants will enjoy a vacation outside in summer.

DRY, CRISPY LEAVES AT THE BASE?

This is just a case of the older leaves dying off. It is normal and nothing to worry about.

♥ SAVE IT *Gently pull the dead leaves away.*

BLEACHED OR BROWN PATCHES ON LEAVES?

This may be sunburn, or rot from where water droplets have gathered on the leaves.

♥ SAVE IT *Move your plant out of direct sunlight. Don't splash the leaves—water from below if necessary (see Water it, pp.18–19).*

BUG ALERT!
(see pp.24–27)

Prone to **mealybugs** on the foliage, and, if the plant has been outside in summer, **vine weevil** grubs in the potting mix.

YELLOW, TRANSLUCENT, OR SOGGY LEAVES?

This is most likely a sign of overwatering, and, if not dealt with, can lead to the plant rotting.

❤ **SAVE IT** *Reduce watering and check that the potting mix and pot are well drained.*

LEAVES SHRIVELING?

Your plant needs water.

❤ **SAVE IT** *Water your plant lightly over a few days—the leaves should soon become plump again.*

SHARE THE CARE

AEONIUM
Aeonium
Care for these rosette-forming succulents in the same way as echeveria. They come in a wide range of colors.

TIGER'S JAW
Faucaria
Care for this succulent in the same way. Don't worry about the spiny-looking edges to the leaves—they're not sharp.

Echeveria secunda var. 'Glauca'
Height & spread: up to 4in (10cm)

POINSETTIA
Euphorbia pulcherrima

The red bracts of poinsettias give them
a festive feel. Exposure to cold can kill them,
so wrap them up well to take them home.

HOW NOT TO KILL IT

LOCATION
Keep the plant in a warm, bright
spot, away from cold drafts or heat registers,
in a room that is 65–73°F (15–23°C).
Maintain a constant temperature.

LIGHT
Place it in bright light, away from
direct sun.

WATERING + FEEDING
Water so that the potting mix is
moist, but not soggy. Allow the top ½–¾in
(1–2cm) of mix to dry out before watering
again. Let any excess water drain away.

CARE
A more humid atmosphere will make
the bracts last longer, so keep plants away
from heat sources, such as space heaters.

Pale bract

PALE LEAVES AND BRACTS?

This happens naturally with age.
It could be that your plant isn't getting
enough sunlight or is too hot.

SAVE IT *Move your plant to a
brighter spot. If in a room warmer than
73°F (23°C), move somewhere cooler.*

BROWN TIPS OR EDGES ON LEAVES OR BRACTS?

The air is too dry.

SAVE IT *Mist the leaves frequently,
especially if the plant is in a heated room.*

**BUG
ALERT!**
(see pp.24–27)

Prone to **mealybugs**
and **spider mites**
on the foliage.

YELLOWING, DROPPING LEAVES?

Your plant could be too hot and dry, or it might not be getting enough light or water.

❤ **SAVE IT** *Check that your plant isn't near a heat source and has enough bright light. Water the plant if the potting mix is dry.*

NO MORE BRACTS?

The bracts will fade in spring, but you can try to make your plant reflower the following year.

❤ **SAVE IT** *During midspring, prune it back to about 4in (10cm) in height, repot, and water. In summer, keep your plant in a cool spot with bright, indirect light (about 60°F/15°C). In early fall, put your plant in a closet or cover it with a black plastic bag for 14 hours each night for 10 weeks. Don't forget to take it out during the day. It should flower again for the festive season.*

Euphorbia pulcherrima

Height & spread: up to 24in (60cm)

PLANT WILTING AND/OR LOSING ITS LEAVES?

Leaf loss often follows wilting. It could be due to exposure to cold or cold drafts, under- or overwatering, or a sudden change in conditions.

❤ **SAVE IT** *Soak underwatered plants in lukewarm water for an hour—they should revive quickly. Check overwatered plants for root rot and remove affected areas (see Plant diseases, pp.28–29). Allow the potting mix to dry out before you water again. Make sure your plant is in a warm spot, free of drafts. Your plant is likely to die if it has been exposed to cold.*

FIDDLE-LEAF FIG
Ficus lyrata

A lush, exotic tree that brings a sense of the jungle to your living room.

Whole plant

HOW NOT TO KILL IT

LOCATION
Choose a bright spot in a warmish room (64–75°F/18–24°C), away from any heat registers or drafts, and no colder than 55°F (13°C) in winter. The plant doesn't like being moved, so once you have found the right spot for it, leave it there.

LIGHT
Place it in bright light, but direct summer sun will burn the leaves.

WATERING + FEEDING
From spring to fall, water only when the top 1in (2–3cm) of mix is dry. Water sparingly during winter. Feed monthly in spring and summer.

CARE
Clean the leaves if dusty. Mist them occasionally—more in summer, or if the room is heated. You might need to support the plant with a cane. When the plant is young, repot it into a slightly larger pot every spring. As it matures, replace only the top 2in (5cm) of potting mix.

BUG ALERT!
(see pp.24–27)

Prone to **mealybugs**, **scale insects**, and **spider mites** on the foliage.

SUDDEN LEAF LOSS?

A sudden loss of a lot of leaves could be due to your plant being moved, which will cause it stress. Alternatively, it could be caused by dry air, over- or underwatering, over- or underfeeding, temperature, and drafts.

SAVE IT *Avoid moving your plant. If your plant has not recently been moved, check its location and your care regimen.*

LEAF TIPS TURNING BROWN?

This is probably due to low humidity, or inadequate or erratic watering.

☀ **SAVE IT** *Move away from any heat sources and drafts. Make sure you water at regular intervals, and check that the whole root ball gets wet.*

Ficus lyrata

Height: up to 10ft (3m)

Spread: up to 3ft (1m)

Leaf spot

DARK PATCHES OR SPOTS ON LEAVES?

Dark patches could be sunburn. Small dark spots could be leaf spot.

☀ **SAVE IT** *Move it out of direct sunlight. If leaf spot, remove any affected leaves and treat with fungicide (see Plant diseases, pp.28–29).*

SHARE THE CARE

WEEPING FIG
Ficus benjamina
Care for this fig as you would a fiddle-leaf fig—keep it away from drafts and heat registers, and try not to move it.

RUBBER PLANT
Ficus elastica
An easy-care alternative to the fiddle-leaf fig. Wipe the leaves frequently and don't overwater.

NERVE PLANT
Fittonia

Found in Peruvian rainforests, nerve plants are grown for their strikingly patterned leaves, further enhanced in the species shown by their pinky-red veining.

HOW NOT TO KILL IT

LOCATION
This plant loves warmth, so put it in a room that is 60–75°F (15–23°C). A spot in a bathroom or kitchen could be ideal if the temperature is consistent. The nerve plant is also well suited to being grown in a terrarium.

LIGHT
Place it in a partially shaded spot as it doesn't like bright sunlight—most windowsills are probably too bright.

WATERING + FEEDING
From spring to fall, water generously with lukewarm water when the top 1/2in (1cm) of potting mix is dry, making sure that the excess water drains away. Water less in winter and don't let the plant sit in cold, wet potting mix.

CARE
Set the plant on a pebble-filled tray of water and mist the leaves daily to ensure that it has enough humidity.

Fittonia verschaffeltii
Height: up to 6in (15cm)
Spread: indefinite

BUG ALERT!
(see pp.24–27)

Prone to **aphids**.

Aphids on the underside of a young leaf

PLANT HAS COLLAPSED?

Nerve plants are prone to collapsing dramatically if their potting mix is too dry.

☀ **SAVE IT** *Water well and mist the leaves. Ensure that you water your plant correctly (see left). If the potting mix has been dry for a long time, your plant may not recover.*

LEAF TIPS TURNING BROWN?

This is due to low humidity.

☀ **SAVE IT** *Mist the leaves regularly and set your plant on a pebble-filled tray of water.*

YELLOW LEAVES?

This is probably due to overwatering.

☀ **SAVE IT** *Nerve plants like moisture, but not soggy potting mix. Remove the yellowed leaves and ensure that you allow the mix to dry out between waterings.*

Yellowing leaves

SHARE THE CARE

PURPLE PASSION
Gynura aurantiaca
It's hard to resist stroking this plant's velvety leaves. It has similar needs to a nerve plant, but likes bright light.

POLKA-DOT PLANT
Hypoestes
This plant has similar needs to the nerve plant, but can take more bright light. It is good for a terrarium.

ENGLISH IVY
Hedera helix

Unlike many houseplants, ivy does best in cool temperatures, so this tough, trailing plant should be used as an attractive addition to a colder room.

HOW NOT TO KILL IT

LOCATION
Place it in a cool or even cold room (35–60°F/2–16°C). It should be grown up a pole, planted in a hanging planter, or could be placed in a pot on a shelf. It's good for unheated porches or drafty hallways.

LIGHT
Provide bright but indirect light. Nonvariegated types will tolerate lower light levels.

WATERING + FEEDING
From spring to fall, keep the potting mix moist, but not wet, watering when the top 1in (2–3cm) of potting mix is dry. Water more sparingly in winter. Feed monthly in spring and summer.

CARE
Mist the plant on warm days. Repot in spring when the roots have filled the pot.

SPINDLY GROWTH?

The room is too warm, or your plant isn't getting enough light.

☀ **SAVE IT** *Move your plant to a cool, bright spot. Cut off the affected areas to encourage more bushy growth.*

Hedera helix
Height & spread: up to 1ft (30cm)

BROWN LEAF TIPS OR EDGES?

This happens if the air around your plant is too warm and dry.

☀ **SAVE IT** *Move your plant to a cooler, more humid spot, especially if it is in a heated room or if the weather is warm.*

Dry, brown leaf edges

VARIEGATED LEAVES TURNING ALL GREEN?

Your plant isn't getting enough light.

☀ **SAVE IT** *Move it to a brighter spot.*

Leaves have lost variegation

Signs of spider mites

BUG ALERT! (see pp.24–27) | Prone to **spider mites** on the foliage.

SHARE THE CARE

SPOTTED LAUREL
Aucuba japonica
Care for this evergreen shrub in the same way as English ivy. It's great for a cool spot, such as a porch or hallway.

JAPANESE ARALIA
Fatsia japonica
An evergreen shrub that can be cared for in the same way as English ivy.

AMARYLLIS
Hippeastrum

Often sold in a kit, these bulbs will produce striking flowers year after year with the right care.

HOW NOT TO KILL IT

LOCATION
Keep the planted bulb in a bright spot that's around 68°F (20°C) and away from drafts. Once it's in flower, you could move it to a slightly cooler spot to prolong the flowers.

LIGHT
Place it in bright light and keep out of direct sun.

WATERING + FEEDING
Keep the potting mix moist, but not soggy. Feed once a month.

CARE
Amaryllis is often sold in a planting kit with potting mix and a pot. Plant the bulb in fall or winter, ensuring that the pot isn't much larger than the bulb. Use multipurpose potting mix and add perlite for drainage. Don't bury the whole bulb—the neck and "shoulders" should be above the mix. It should flower 6–8 weeks after planting. Turn the pot regularly to prevent the plant from growing toward the light.

BUG ALERT!
(see pp.24–27)

Prone to **mealybugs** on or under the leaves and around the plant.

NO MORE FLOWERS?

Amaryllis flowers will fade in spring, but it is possible to get them to reflower the following winter or spring.

SAVE IT *After flowering, cut off the spent flower spike to about 2in (5cm) above the bulb and feed and water as usual. You could put the plant outside in summer. In early fall, give the plant a rest period in a room at 50–55°F (10–13°C). Stop feeding and reduce watering during this time. The foliage will die back. After 8–10 weeks of rest, replace the top 2in (5cm) of the potting mix, bring back into a warm room, and feed and water as before. It should then flower 6–8 weeks later.*

Hippeastrum
Height: up to 24in (60cm).
Spread: up to 12in (30cm)

FLOWER SPIKE SLOW TO DEVELOP?

You may have the plant in too cool a room.

☀ **SAVE IT** *Move it to a warmer spot (around 68°F/20°C). Check that the potting mix is moist, but not soggy.*

NO FLOWER THE FOLLOWING WINTER?

This may be because your plant has not rested for long enough in the right conditions.

☀ **SAVE IT** *Make sure that the rest period is 8–10 weeks and you are providing enough light and the correct care (see No more flowers?).*

KENTIA PALM
Howea fosteriana

Popular since the 19th century, this low-maintenance palm brings an air of elegance to your home.

....

HOW NOT TO KILL IT

 LOCATION
Provide temperatures of 64–75°F (18–24°C), and a minimum temperature of 54°F (12°C) in winter. It should be kept away from heat sources.

 LIGHT
Place it in bright, but indirect light. Direct sun will scorch the leaves.

 WATERING + FEEDING
Water in spring and summer so the potting mix is moist, but allow it to dry out slightly in between. Reduce watering in winter. Feed monthly in spring and summer.

CARE
Clean the leaves regularly—you could put it under a lukewarm shower, or in summer rain. Only repot when roots are visible above the potting mix or growing through the drainage holes. The roots are delicate and easily damaged, so handle carefully when repotting.

Whole plant

LEAF TIPS GOING BROWN?

A hot, dry room can cause brown leaf tips. So can drafts, underwatering, or overwatering.

💜 **SAVE IT** *If the plant is near a heat register, move it away. Check that the temperature isn't too low and water if the potting mix is dry. Cut off the brown tips with scissors just inside the brown area.*

BUG ALERT!
(see pp.24–27)

Prone to **scale insects**, **mealybugs**, and **spider mites** on the foliage.

DULL LEAVES?

A lack of shine on the leaves can be caused by low humidity.

❤ **SAVE IT** *Keep it away from heat registers and mist the leaves frequently.*

YELLOWING LEAVES?

Yellow lower leaves can be due to age. If widespread, it could be a sign of over- or underwatering, cold drafts, underfeeding, or the plant is root-bound.

❤ **SAVE IT** *Check your care regime (see left).*

LEAVES GOING BROWN?

Old, lower leaves naturally turn brown and die, but check whether the plant doesn't need repotting or is waterlogged.

❤ **SAVE IT** *Cut any unsightly brown leaves off at the base using pruners. Check your watering regimen (see left).*

Howea fosteriana
Height: up to 10ft (3m)
Spread: up to 32in (80cm)

SHARE THE CARE

PARLOR PALM
Chamaedorea elegans
An easy-to-grow palm with the same care as Kentia palm. It is compact, only reaching about 3ft (1m).

BUTTERFLY PALM
Dypsis lutescens
Another, similar palm with the same care needs. It likes good light and a slightly humid atmosphere.

TOP 5 PLANTS FOR
THE BATHROOM

Plants can add a lush, verdant feel to your bathroom. Many plants love the high humidity produced by bathtubs and showers. Here are five beautiful specimens to try.

Nerve plant
Fittonia

This rainforest plant has beautiful, veined foliage. It loves high humidity, so is perfect for a bathroom. Keep it in a partially shaded spot.

See Nerve plant, pp.78–79.

Maidenhair fern
Adiantum raddianum

If you take plenty of baths and showers, your maidenhair fern will be happy, as it enjoys a humid atmosphere. It has pleasing, delicate foliage.

See Maidenhair fern, p.105.

Purple passion
Gynura aurantiaca

This pretty foliage plant has soft, velvety leaves. It will begin to trail once the plant matures. It likes humidity and bright light, so put it within a few feet of a bathroom window.

See Purple passion, p.79.

Boston fern
Nephrolepis exaltata

The Boston fern thrives in a room with high humidity, making it a good choice for a bathroom. The arching fronds look particularly good in a hanging planter.

See Boston fern, p.93.

Wax flower
Hoya carnosa

This climbing plant has beautiful, waxy flowers, and its evening scent is perfect for a relaxing bathtime. It requires lots of light and humidity, so needs to be kept in a bright bathroom.

See Wax flower, pp.88–89.

WAX FLOWER
Hoya carnosa

This climbing plant, also known as the Hindu rope plant, has pretty flowers that are especially scented in the evening.

Whole plant

HOW NOT TO KILL IT

LOCATION
Grow it up a trellis or pole, keeping it at 64–75°F (18–24°C) and above 50°F (10°C) in winter. It can get quite large, so it will need plenty of space.

LIGHT
Place it in a bright spot, out of direct sun, which can scorch the leaves.

WATERING + FEEDING
From spring to fall, water when the top 1in (2–3cm) of potting mix dries out, making the mix moist, but not wet. Keep almost dry in winter. Feed monthly from spring to late summer.

CARE
Use well-drained potting mix. To add humidity, set the plant on a pebble-filled tray of water. Mist the leaves—more often in a hot room. Don't mist, move, or repot the plant when it is in bud or flower. Remove the top 2in (5cm) of potting mix and replace with fresh each spring. Only repot if it's completely pot-bound. Don't deadhead the plant or cut off the flowering stalks as these will reflower.

DROPPING FLOWER BUDS?

The potting mix may be too dry or wet, or you may have moved or repotted your plant while it was in bud.

SAVE IT *Avoid moving your plant while it is in bud or flower. Check your watering regimen (see left).*

NO FLOWERS?

Your plant may not be in a bright enough spot—it can survive low light levels, but won't flower. You may have removed the flowering stalks.

SAVE IT *Move it to a brighter spot. Each stalk can produce flowers for many years, so be sure not to deadhead—let the spent flowers fall off naturally.*

BUG ALERT!
(see pp.24–27)

Prone to **mealybugs, whiteflies, scale insects**, and **aphids**.

SHARE THE CARE

MINIATURE WAX PLANT
Hoya bella
This is a more compact plant that has similar care needs as a wax flower, but likes a higher temperature (no less than 60°F/16°C in winter).

DRIPPING FLOWERS?

The flowers produce nectar to attract pollinators—this is normal.

☀ SAVE IT
Do nothing!

BLACKENED, YELLOWING, OR DROPPING LEAVES?

This could be due to overwatering, or excessive cold in winter.

☀ SAVE IT *Check that the potting mix isn't waterlogged. Water more sparingly. Move the plant if it is too cold.*

Blackened leaf ←

Hoya carnosa 'Variegata'

Height: up to 13ft (4m)

Spread: up to 28in (70cm)

KALANCHOE
Kalanchoe blossfeldiana

These succulent plants are sold all year round and have long-lasting red, pink, orange, white, or yellow flowers.

BUG ALERT!
(see pp.24–27)

Prone to **mealybugs** and **spider mites** on the foliage.

HOW NOT TO KILL IT

LOCATION
Keep it at 65–75°F (18–24°C), and above 50°F (10°C) in winter.

LIGHT
Place it in bright light, including some direct sun—close to an east- or west-facing window in spring or summer, and a south-facing one in winter.

WATERING + FEEDING
Water when the top 1in (2–3cm) of potting mix is dry, but more sparingly in winter. Make sure the pot has good drainage so the plant isn't sitting in soggy mix. If you keep the plant after it has flowered, feed it once a month in spring and summer.

CARE
Pinch off the flowers as they fade. After flowering, cut back all the flowered stems. Most people discard their plant after flowering, but it is possible to make it flower again if you follow a specific care regimen (see No more flowers?).

NO MORE FLOWERS?
The flowers will fade after around 8 weeks, but you can try to get your plant to flower again.

☀ **SAVE IT** *Put your plant outside in summer, then bring it indoors in fall as temperatures start to fall. Place in a cool but bright location, stopping feeding, and watering less. It will then need 14 hours of darkness each night for at least a month to reflower—place it in a closet every evening if it is in a room with artificial light. Resume feeding and watering around 8 weeks later when the plant forms flower buds.*

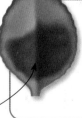

BROWN PATCHES ON LEAVES?
This is probably sunburn.

☀ **SAVE IT** *Move your plant so that it receives less direct sunlight.*

Brown patches

LEAVES HAVE A RED EDGE?

This is nothing to worry about—the leaves turn red if they are in the sun.

☀ **SAVE IT** *Your plant is happy, but watch for sunburn on the leaves.*

PLANT WILTING?

Your plant may have gotten too cold, or it might be over- or underwatered.

❤ **SAVE IT** *Move it to a warmer spot (such as away from a windowsill that gets too cold at night) and out of cold drafts. Check your watering regimen (see left).*

SHARE THE CARE

CALANDIVA
Kalanchoe
Calandiva® series
Bears masses of small, rose-like, fully double flowers. Treat in exactly the same way as you would a Kalanchoe.

Kalanchoe blossfeldiana

Height: up to 12in (30cm)

Spread: up to 8in (20cm)

STEM TURNED BROWN OR BLACK AND MUSHY?

This is stem rot, due to overwatering.

☀ **SAVE IT** *Remove affected areas of the plant. For more information, see Plant diseases (pp.28–29).*

Black and mushy stem

CROCODILE FERN
Microsorum musifolium

With leaves like crinkly crocodile skin, the crocodile fern is perfect for a kitchen or bathroom, where it will enjoy the humidity.

HOW NOT TO KILL IT

LOCATION
Keep at 55–75°F (13–24°C) and away from heat sources, such as space heaters.

LIGHT
Place it in light shade away from direct sunlight. Move the plant closer to a window in winter if light levels are very low.

WATERING + FEEDING
Let the top layer of potting mix almost dry out between waterings from spring to early fall. In winter, let the top layer dry out completely, then water.

CARE
Repot when root-bound with a mix of soil-based and multipurpose potting mix.

PALE, YELLOWING LEAVES?

Your fern is getting too much light.

💜 **SAVE IT** *Move the plant to a shadier spot.*

A MUSHY CROWN OR STEMS?

These mushy parts of the plant are rotting.

💜 **SAVE IT** *Carefully avoid watering over the center of the plant to make sure water does not collect and sit in the crown, where it will cause it to rot.*

SHARE THE CARE

BOSTON FERN
Nephrolepis exaltata **'Bostoniensis'**
This classic fern needs the potting mix moist at all times and benefits from a monthly feed from spring to fall.

BUG ALERT!
(see pp.24–27)

Scale and **mealybug** can be a problem.

Monstera deliciosa
Height & spread: up to 24in (60cm)

CRISPY LEAVES?

This can be a sign of underwatering or air that is too dry.

💜 **SAVE IT** *Increase watering and move the plant away from any heat sources to a spot with higher humidity, such as a bathroom or kitchen.*

BIRD'S NEST FERN
Asplenium nidus
This fern produces a spreading rosette of leaves thought to resemble a bird's nest. Wipe the leaves to keep them shiny. It copes well with lower light levels.

SENSITIVE PLANT
Mimosa pudica

This plant has a charming party trick—
when you touch it, its leaves fold up and
its stems droop.

HOW NOT TO KILL IT

LOCATION
Keep it at 64–75°F (18–24°C),
and above 60°F (15°C) in winter.

LIGHT
Provide plenty of bright light,
including some direct sun.

WATERING + FEEDING
Keep the potting mix moist, but not
soggy, and just moist in winter. Feed once
a month during spring and summer.

CARE
Sensitive plants like humidity, so
place the plant on a pebble-filled tray of
water. Often sold in a planting kit, they are
easy to grow from seed. It will produce
pretty, pink flowers in summer.

PLANT REACTS SLOWLY WHEN TOUCHED AND IS SLOW TO RECOVER?

You've been touching it too
much, making it less "ticklish."
After being touched, the leaves
can take up to half an hour
to unfold.

☀ **SAVE IT** *Give your plant
a break from being touched for a
while—it might need several weeks
to become sensitized again.*

*Leaves
when open*

*Leaves
when closed*

> **BUG ALERT!**
> (see pp.24–27)
>
> Prone to
> **spider mites**
> on the foliage.

Whole plant

PLANT GETTING LARGE AND LEGGY?

This is normal. The plant becomes less attractive over time, and most people discard their plant in fall, after it has finished flowering.

❤ **SAVE IT** *Cut it back to the desired size, or sow or buy a new plant in spring.*

LEAVES CLOSED BUT THE PLANT HASN'T BEEN TOUCHED?

The plant can react if shaken or brushed by a breeze. The leaves will also fold up naturally at night.

❤ **SAVE IT** *Do nothing!*

LEAVES TURNING YELLOW AND FALLING OFF?

Your plant is probably too cold.

❤ **SAVE IT** *Move it to a warmer spot.*

Mimosa pudica

Height: up to 2ft (60cm)

Spread: up to 1ft (30cm)

SPLIT-LEAF PHILODENDRON
Monstera deliciosa

A 1970s favorite, this plant will instantly give any room a fun, jungle look.

HOW NOT TO KILL IT

 LOCATION
It will survive at 50–75°F (10–24°C), but will only grow if over 65°F (18°C). Provide space as it can get pretty large.

 LIGHT
Place it in a bright or lightly shaded spot, such as a few feet from a window. Keep out of direct sunlight.

 WATERING + FEEDING
Water after the top of the potting mix has dried out a little. Feed once a month during spring and summer.

CARE
Wipe the leaves occasionally to keep them free of dust, and mist them from time to time. Once the plant reaches 30in (75cm) tall, it will need support, such as a moss pole or bamboo cane. Tuck the long aerial roots into the potting mix or the pole. Repot every spring when young. When your plant gets too big to repot easily, remove the top 2in (5cm) of potting mix and replace with fresh.

YELLOW LEAVES?

Overwatering is the most likely cause, especially if they are also wilting, which may have led to root rot. Or the plant may need feeding. The lower, small leaves will naturally turn yellow as they age and is nothing to worry about.

SAVE IT *Reduce watering. Feed your plant once a month in spring and summer. Check for root rot, removing any affected roots. For more information, see Plant diseases (pp.28–29).*

LEAF TIPS AND EDGES TURNING BROWN?

This may be due to dry air or potting mix, low temperatures, or because your plant has become pot-bound.

SAVE IT *If your plant is in a warm room (over 75°F/24°C) with dry air, set it on a pebble-filled tray of water and mist the leaves regularly. If it is near a heat register, move it away. Check that the room isn't too cold. Repot if necessary.*

THE PLANT IS "CRYING?"

Water will sometimes drip from leaves after watering; known as guttation, it is generally nothing to worry about.

☀ **SAVE IT** *If you notice this happening a lot, check that you are not overwatering your plant.*

BUG ALERT!
(see pp.24–27)

Prone to **mealybugs** on the undersides of leaves.

UNCUT LEAVES?

Young plants and new stems do not produce cut leaves. Uncut leaves on mature stems are a sign your plant is unhappy.

☀ **SAVE IT** *If you have a young plant, be patient! If not, make sure your plant is in a good location that is over 65°F (18°C) and you are providing the correct watering, feeding, and care (see left).*

Monstera deliciosa
Height & spread: up to 6ft (1.8m)

SHARE THE CARE

XANADU PHILODENDRON
Thaumatophyllum xanadu
The luscious dome of dark green leaves helps this recently renamed philodendron tolerate very low light levels. Keep it between 60–75°F (15–24°C) and repot every two to three years.

SWISS CHEESE VINE
Monstera adansonii
With the same care demands as a Split-leaf philodendron, this variety has unusual, oval holes in its leaves.

BUNNY EARS CACTUS
Opuntia microdasys

Beware the fine hairs of the bunny ears cactus. They might look soft, but these prickles are painfully irritating if they become lodged in the skin.

HOW NOT TO KILL IT

 LOCATION
Put this cactus somewhere warm (55–85°F/13–29°C). In winter, move it to a cooler spot to encourage flowers, but never let it freeze.

 LIGHT
Place it in full sun all year round and provide air circulation on hot days.

 WATERING + FEEDING
In spring and summer, let the top ¾in (2cm) of the potting mix dry out before watering. Keep the potting mix almost dry in fall and totally dry in winter. Feed once a month from spring to fall.

CARE
Grow in cactus potting mix. Wear thorn-proof gloves when handling this plant; the hairs may look soft, but they are painfully irritating and difficult to remove.

BUG ALERT!
(see pp.24–27) | Prone to **mealybugs**, **scale insects**, and **red spider mites**.

SHRIVELING LEAVES?

This is due to underwatering. Contrary to popular opinion, cacti do need watering!

SAVE IT *Water the potting mix a small amount every day for the next few days, but don't let the plant sit in wet potting mix.*

MUSHY PLANT?

The mushy parts of the plant have rotted. This is due to overwatering, often combined with low temperatures.

SAVE IT *Depending on how far the rot has spread, you could try repotting your plant into fresh cactus potting mix. Cut away any rotted roots.*

NO FLOWERS?

It is possible to coax some cacti into flowering (such as *Mammillaria*, *Opuntia*, *Astrophytum*, and *Rebutia*) when they are a few years old.

☀ **SAVE IT** *Stop watering in fall, then in winter, place your plant in a cool, light room and keep the potting mix dry. In spring, bring into a warmer spot before resuming gentle watering and feeding. Keeping the plant in a small pot will also encourage it to flower.*

BROWN/WHITE DISCOLORATION?

This is sunburn and occurs if the plant is in very strong sunlight.

☀ **SAVE IT** *Move your plant out of very strong midday sun in summer.*

CACTUS SPLITTING?

This is due to overwatering.

☀ **SAVE IT** *Stop watering—the scar should heal over. Check your watering regime (see left). Also check that the potting mix and pot are well-drained.*

Opuntia microdasys
Height: up to 18in (45cm)
Spread: up to 24in (60cm)

SHARE THE CARE

MONK'S HOOD
Astrophytum ornatum
This small cactus has a round shape and can produce yellow flowers.

CROWN CACTUS
Rebutia
This popular cactus produces pretty, tubular flowers close to its base.

WATERMELON PEPEROMIA
Peperomia argyreia

An easy-to-care-for tropical beauty, this species of peperomia has dark green, patterned leaves that resemble the skin of a watermelon.

....

HOW NOT TO KILL IT

 LOCATION
Provide temperatures of 60–75°F (15–24°C) during the growing season from spring to fall and a minimum temperature of 50°F (10°C) in winter.

 LIGHT
Place in bright light, out of direct sun.

 WATERING + FEEDING
Water with lukewarm water from spring to fall whenever the potting mix is beginning to dry out. Reduce watering to almost nothing in winter. Feed monthly in spring and summer.

CARE
It needs good drainage but likes being root-bound, so you can wait a good three years before repotting.

Peperomia argyreia.
Height & spread: up to 8in (20cm)

> **BUG ALERT!**
> (see pp.24–27)
> | Prone to **mealybugs** under the leaves and around the plant.

Corky swellings

CORKY SWELLINGS UNDER THE LEAVES?

This is a disorder called edema, caused by too much watering in winter.

♥ **SAVE IT** *Ensure you water your plant sparingly in winter. For more information, see Plant diseases (pp.28–29).*

see Plant diseases (pp.28–29)

LEAF DROP?

This can be caused by a lack of water, or if the plant is too cold.

♥ **SAVE IT** *Water your plant. If it is located in a room cooler than 50°F (10°C), move it to a warmer spot.*

PLANT WILTING DESPITE WATERING?

You may have overwatered your plant, causing root rot.

♥ **SAVE IT** *Check your plant for root rot and remove any affected areas. For more information, see Plant diseases (pp.28–29).*

see Plant diseases (pp.28–29)

SHARE THE CARE

CREEPING BUTTONS
Peperomia rotundifolia
A pretty, trailing peperomia with small, fleshy, buttonlike leaves. Keep it in moderate to high humidity.

RAINDROP PEPEROMIA
Peperomia polybotrya
This plant has gorgeous glossy, heart-shaped leaves. It also likes higher humidity than the watermelon peperomia.

MOTH ORCHID
Phalaenopsis

The orchid family is enormous. Moth orchids are the easiest to grow, and their flowers last for many weeks.

HOW NOT TO KILL IT

LOCATION
Place the plant in a room with a temperature of around 65–80°F (18–26°C).

LIGHT
Put it in bright but indirect light—near an east-facing window is ideal.

WATERING + FEEDING
Water by dipping and draining (see Water it, pp.18–19). Do this once a week in spring and summer, and around every 2 weeks in winter. Ideally, use distilled, filtered, or rainwater. Provide orchid fertilizer once a month during spring and summer, but every 2 months in fall and winter.

CARE
Grow in orchid potting mix in a transparent container so that light can reach the roots. Don't cut off or cover the roots that are sticking into the air—they will rot. Once the flowers fade, cut back the flowering stem to a bud lower down, and it should produce a new flower spike within a few months.

BUD DROP
This could be due to under- or overwatering, low humidity, or temperature fluctuation.

SAVE IT *Water normally (see left), and place your plant on a pebble-filled tray of water. Avoid moving your plant when it is in bud.*

BUG ALERT!
(see pp.24–27)

Prone to **scale insects** and **mealybugs** on the foliage.

Phalaenopsis
Height: up to 3ft (1m)
Spread: up to 12in (30cm)

NO FLOWERS?

It may take several months for your plant to reflower. However, a lack of flowers can also be due to a lack of bright light, over- or underfeeding, or excessive temperature fluctuations. Your plant may need repotting.

💗 **SAVE IT** *Move your plant to a brighter spot, making sure you feed it monthly in spring and summer and every 2 months in fall and winter. Repot if necessary. Lower nighttime temperatures (55–65°F/13–18°C) can stimulate reflowering, so put it on a windowsill or in a cooler room for a few weeks.*

CHANGE IN LEAF COLOR?

The leaves should be a grassy green. Yellowing of older leaves is natural, but for younger leaves, it can be a sign of too much bright sunlight or underfeeding. The leaves becoming darker can be a sign of a lack of bright sunlight.

Yellow leaves

💗 **SAVE IT** *Adjust the plant's light levels accordingly. If it is spring or summer, make sure you feed your plant once a month.*

Shriveled leaves

SHRIVELED LEAVES?

This probably means that not enough water is reaching the leaves. This is often due to underwatering, but can be caused by root damage. Limp leaves could also be a sign that there is not enough humidity.

💗 **SAVE IT** *Healthy roots are silvery or green, while brown, mushy roots indicate overwatering and hollow, crispy roots are a sign of underwatering. If roots are damaged, trim off the worst of the damage and repot in fresh potting mix. Raise the humidity by setting your plant on a pebble-filled tray of water.*

BLUE STAR FERN
Phlebodium aureum

This plant is one of the easier-to-care-for ferns. It has a lovely blue-green color with cartoonishly lobed fronds.

HOW NOT TO KILL IT

LOCATION
Position it away from drafts and heat sources in a room that is 50–70°F (10–21°C). A room with high humidity would be ideal.

LIGHT
This fern likes to be in full or partial shade and well away from direct sunlight.

WATERING + FEEDING
Keep the potting mix moist but well drained. Feed monthly when in growth.

CARE
Remove any old fronds at the base. Repot when the roots fill the pot.

THE FRONDS ARE TURNING YELLOW?

This may be a sign of root rot.

SAVE IT *Inspect the roots for rot. Remove any brown or mushy ones and their surrounding soil. Make sure drainage is adequate and that the soil is moist but not wet from watering.*

BUG ALERT!
(see pp.24–27)

Prone to **scale insects** and **mealybugs** on the foliage.

LEAF TIPS BROWN?

The air is too hot or dry. It may also need more water.

💚 **SAVE IT** *Move the plant away from any drafts, heat sources, or intense sunlight. If possible, move it to a room with higher humidity, such as a bathroom or kitchen. Increase watering if necessary.*

SHARE THE CARE

CRETAN BRAKE FERN
Pteris cretica

This fern produces unusual, almost palmlike foliage and is more forgiving than many ferns if the potting mix dries out occasionally.

Phlebodium aureum
Height and spread: up to 3ft (1m)

LOSING LEAVES?

Leaf fall can result from both under- and overwatering.

💚 **SAVE IT** *Check that the soil is not wet or drying out completely, but moist and well drained.*

MAIDENHAIR FERN
Adiantum raddianum

This delicate, arching fern can be fussy to grow. It prefers to be kept between 60–70°F (15–21°C) and should be watered when the top ½in (1cm) potting mix is dry, letting the excess drain away.

TOP 5 PLANTS FOR
LOW
LIGHT

All plants need some light in order to grow, but some plants, especially those with larger leaves, are better at coping with a shadier spot. Here are five of the best shady characters to try.

Bird's nest fern
Asplenium nidus

This easy-care fern has a rosette of lush, shiny leaves. It copes well in low light, but wipe the leaves occasionally to keep them shiny and allow light to get to them.

See Bird's nest fern, p.93.

Peace lily
Spathiphyllum

Peace lilies are forgiving plants with glossy green leaves and striking white flowers. They don't mind low light levels and can also put up with erratic watering.

See Peace lily, pp.124–125.

Heart-leaf philodendron
Philodendron scandens

This philodendron has glossy, heart-shaped leaves. It's a climber, so train it up a mossy pole.

See Heart-leaf philodendron, p.109.

Japanese aralia
Fatsia japonica

This striking plant, with its large, lush, glossy leaves, copes well in low light levels and can survive temperatures as low as 32°F (0°C) in winter.

See Japanese aralia, p.81.

Cast iron plant
Aspidistra elatior

As its name suggests, this plant has a strong constitution. Wipe the leaves to allow maximum light to get to them. It's forgiving of underwatering, but it has one pet peeve: very wet potting mix.

See Cast iron plant, p.125.

IMPERIAL RED PHILODENDRON
Philodendron 'Imperial Red'

This philodendron has large, waxy leaves that emerge red when young and gradually darken to purple and then dark green.

HOW NOT TO KILL IT

 LOCATION
This plant likes moderate temperatures between 60–75°F (15–24°C).

 LIGHT
Place it in a bright spot, away from direct sunlight.

 WATERING + FEEDING
Water whenever the top 1in (2–3cm) of potting mix is dry. Water sparingly in winter. Feed once a month in spring and summer.

 CARE
These glossy leaves easily collect dust. Remove it with a damp cloth regularly. Repot in spring.

BUG ALERT!
(see pp.24–27)

Scale insect and **red spider mites** can be a problem.

WILTING OR YELLOWING LEAVES?

You are probably overwatering your plant.

☀ **SAVE IT** *This plant does not like overly wet soil. Make sure that the top layer of potting mix is allowed to dry out between watering and that the pot is draining well.*

LEAVES ARE FALLING?

The room may be too cold or drafty for your plant.

☀ **SAVE IT** *Move it to a place where temperatures are more moderate, away from cold drafts of air.*

LEAF EDGES TURNING BROWN?

This is a sign that your plant is losing water to dry or hot air, not getting enough water, or getting too much sunlight.

☀ **SAVE IT** *Move the plant away from heat sources, windows, and doors, and make sure the potting mix is not too dry.*

Philodendron 'Imperial Red'

Height: up to 5ft (1.5m)

Spread: up to 3ft (1m)

THE LEAVES ARE LOSING THEIR COLOR?

This philodendron will loose vibrancy if it receives too much bright or direct sunlight.

☀ **SAVE IT** *Check the light levels of the room it is placed in and move it to a shadier spot if necessary.*

SHARE THE CARE

HEART-LEAF PHILODENDRON
Philodendron scandens

Usually sold climbing a moss pole, this glossy-leaved plant can tolerate shady spots. Care for it as you would the Imperial philodendron.

BLUSHING PHILODENDRON
Philodendron erubescens

This slow-growing climber has similar needs. It has purple leaves when young.

CHINESE MONEY PLANT
Pilea peperomioides

This sought-after houseplant is grown
for its pretty, lily pad–like leaves.

HOW NOT TO KILL IT

LOCATION
Keep it in a room that is
64–75°F (18–24°C), but no cooler
than 54°F (12°C) in winter.

LIGHT
Place it in bright light or partial
shade, but avoid direct sunlight, which
will damage the leaves. The leaves will
grow bigger in partial shade than
in bright light.

WATERING +
FEEDING
Keep the potting mix
moist, but let it dry out a little
between waterings. Feed the plant
every 2 weeks in spring and summer.

CARE
Ensure that the plant has good
drainage and don't allow it to sit in wet
potting mix. Occasionally, wipe the leaves
with a clean, damp cloth to keep them dust-
free and shiny. Baby plants will appear at the
base; you can repot them and grow them on.

*Pilea
peperomioides*
Height & spread:
up to 12in
(30cm)

LEAVES FACING IN ONE DIRECTION?

The leaves will grow toward the light.

💙 **SAVE IT** *Rotate your plant regularly so that it keeps its mounded shape.*

LEAVES TURNING YELLOW OR DROPPING OFF?

If the leaves are discoloring at the base of the plant, don't worry—these are just aging leaves. If the problem is widespread, it could be due to root rot. Also check that the plant isn't root-bound.

💙 **SAVE IT** *Check your watering and care regimen (see left).*

BUG ALERT!
(see pp.24–27)

Prone to **scale insects** on the foliage.

CURLING LEAVES?

This means that the plant's conditions aren't quite right.

💙 **SAVE IT** *Check its location and light requirements and tweak your care regime (see left).*

SHARE THE CARE

FRIENDSHIP PLANT
Pilea involucrata
'Moon Valley'
This striking perennial has similar needs to a Chinese money plant, but likes higher humidity. Try keeping it in a terrarium.

ALUMINUM PLANT
Pilea cadierei
This plant can be cared for in the same way as a friendship plant, because it also adores high humidity.

ELKHORN FERN
Platycerium bifurcatum

These ferns grow like air plants in the wild. At home, they can be grown with or without potting mix, and are often sold on a mount.

HOW NOT TO KILL IT

LOCATION
Keep in a humid environment—a bathroom could be ideal. Make sure the temperature is 50–75°F (10–24°C).

LIGHT
Place it in very bright, but indirect light. Direct sunlight will scorch the leaves.

WATERING + FEEDING
Elkhorn ferns absorb water through their roots and fronds. Keep the potting mix lightly moist at all times. To water mounted plants, place them upside down in a bath of lukewarm water and leave for 20 minutes, or run under lukewarm tap water. Drip dry before rehanging. Water weekly if in a hot, dry room, every 2–3 weeks if it is cool or humid. Feed monthly in spring and summer.

CARE
Mist your plant regularly with lukewarm water, especially if it is in a hot, dry room.

> **BUG ALERT!**
> (see pp.24–27)
>
> Prone to **scale insects** on the undersides of the leaves.

Platycerium bifurcatum
Height & spread: up to 3ft (1m)

FROND TIPS BROWNING OR WILTING?

Your plant is not getting enough water.

💙 **SAVE IT** *Water your plant more often and increase humidity by misting the leaves more frequently.*

PLANT WATERED BUT STILL WILTING?

It may have root rot.

💙 **SAVE IT** *Check your plant for root rot and remove any black and mushy roots. For more information, see Plant diseases (pp.28–29).*

SHARE THE CARE

REGAL ELKHORN FERN
Platycerium grande
With pale green, antlerlike fronds, this houseplant is larger than the elkhorn fern, but you can care for it in the same way.

ANTLER FRONDS BROWNING OR BLACKENING AT THE BASE?

This is due to overwatering.

💙 **SAVE IT** *Don't water your plant for a few weeks, then return to a normal watering regimen.*

Antler fronds come from the center

Shield fronds surround the edge

BROWN SHIELD FRONDS?

Elkhorn ferns have small fronds at their base. These are "shield" fronds and help to take up water and protect the roots. They naturally turn brown with age.

💙 **SAVE IT** *Don't do anything—it's a normal process for the lower fronds to turn brown. Don't remove them.*

AFRICAN VIOLET
Saintpaulia

These popular, fuzzy-leaved plants have flowers in a wide range of colors. Their small size makes them ideal if you are short on space.

HOW NOT TO KILL IT

LOCATION
Provide warmth (60–73°F/ 16–23°C) and bright, indirect light.

LIGHT
Place it in bright, indirect light. Shade from direct sunlight, which will scorch the leaves.

WATERING + FEEDING
Water when the top 1in (2–3cm) of potting mix has dried out. The plant should be watered from below for about 30 minutes (see Water it, pp.18–19). This avoids wetting the leaves. Feed once a month from spring to late summer.

CARE
Cut off any spent flowers. African violets grow best in small pots, so don't repot too often.

YELLOW LEAVES?

This could be due to dry air, too much sun, or poor watering or feeding.

☀ **SAVE IT** *Move your plant out of direct sunlight and away from a heat source. Also check your feeding and watering regimen (see left).*

NO FLOWERS?

African violets often stop blooming in winter, due to lower light levels. In spring to fall, a lack of flowers could be due to a care issue.

☀ **SAVE IT** *In winter, move your plant to a bright, south- or west-facing window. If it is spring to fall, check that you are feeding your plant correctly, and that it is in a warm enough location.*

BUG ALERT!
(see pp.24–27)

Prone to **mealybugs** on the undersides of the foliage.

BROWN SPOTS ON LEAVES?

This can happen if the leaves are splashed with water, or your plant is watered with cold water.

SAVE IT *Always water from below to prevent the leaves from being splashed. Stand your plant in a saucer of water for about 30 minutes. Use water that is at room temperature.*

Brown spots

Saintpaulia **'Bright Eyes'**

Height & spread: up to 6in (15cm)

PLANT WILTING?

This is a result of over- or underwatering.

SAVE IT *Ensure you are watering your plant from the bottom when the top 1in (2-3cm) of potting mix has dried out. Check for crown or root rot (see Plant diseases, pp.28–29).*

GRAY FLUFF OR WHITE POWDER ON LEAVES?

Gray fluff is the mold botrytis. White powder is powdery mildew.

SAVE IT *Remove affected areas and treat with fungicide. For more information, see Plant diseases (pp.28–29).*

Gray fluff

SNAKE PLANT
Sansevieria trifasciata

This striking plant with stiff, swordlike leaves is virtually indestructible—the only way to kill it is through overwatering and cold temperatures.

HOW NOT TO KILL IT

LOCATION
A snake plant isn't at all fussy about its location. It will thrive at 50–80°F (10–26°C), and doesn't mind drafts or dry air.

LIGHT
Ideally, provide bright, indirect light, though it will tolerate some direct sun. It will also cope in low light levels, but the variegated leaves may revert to all-green.

WATERING + FEEDING
Water moderately in spring and summer, and sparingly during fall and winter. Feed once a month in spring and summer.

CARE
Grow in a heavy pot to prevent the plant from toppling. Be careful not to damage the leaf tips—this will stop the plant from growing. Wipe the leaves occasionally to keep them shiny. Only repot if pot-bound.

LEAVES FALLING SIDEWAYS?

You may have under- or overwatered your plant, or it isn't getting enough light. It may also be pot-bound. Tall, older leaves do sometimes collapse.

SAVE IT *Check your care regimen and light levels (see left). Repot if necessary.*

YELLOWING LEAVES?

This is usually caused by overwatering, especially during winter. Check the base and roots of your plant for rot.

SAVE IT *Allow the potting mix to dry out. Consider moving your plant to a warmer spot if temperatures are low. Check for root rot, removing any affected roots. For more information, see Plant diseases (pp.28–29).*

Yellow leaf

WRINKLED LEAVES?

If the leaves on your plant are wrinkled, you have probably underwatered it.

💓 **SAVE IT** *Water your plant lightly over a few days and the leaves should firm up again.*

Wrinkled leaf

BUG ALERT!
(see pp.24–27)

Prone to **mealybugs** on the foliage.

Sansevieria trifasciata

Height: up to 4ft (1.2m)

Spread: up to 20in (50cm)

SHARE THE CARE

AFRICAN SPEAR
Sansevieria cylindrica
An African spear has the same care needs as a snake plant. Its cylindrical leaves are often braided.

AFRICAN MILK TREE
Euphorbia trigona
This striking succulent has sharp thorns and the same care requirements.

FOOTSTOOL PALM
Saribus rotundifolius

Grow this architectural palm for its stunning fan-shaped leaves. Outdoors, it can grow up to 65ft (20m); in your home, it may reach 6½ft (2m).

HOW NOT TO KILL IT

LOCATION
This plant will be happiest in a room that stays between 60–75°F (13–24°C). Make sure to give it enough space to grow and spread its leaves.

LIGHT
Place it in bright but indirect sunlight.

WATERING + FEEDING
Wait for the top 1in (3cm) of potting mix to dry out before watering from spring to fall. In the winter, let almost half of the potting mix dry out each time. Feed every month from spring to fall.

CARE
Keep your plant well away from any heat source. Wipe leaves occasionally with a damp cloth to remove any dust.

Saribus rotundifolius
Height: up to 6.5ft (2m)
Spread: up to 3ft (1m)

BUG ALERT!
(see pp.24–27)

Check under leaves and at base of stems for **red spider mites** and **mealybugs**.

BROWN SPOTS ON THE LEAVES?

A symptom of leaf spot disease.

☀ **SAVE IT** *Remove any affected leaves and treat with an organic fungicide.*

LEAVES TURNING YELLOW?

Pale or yellowing leaves are a symptom of underwatering.

☀ **SAVE IT** *Only let the top 1in (3cm) of potting mix dry out in summer and no more, especially if the plant is located in a brighter room.*

BROWN STEMS?

This is a sign of rot, and it can be caused by a combination of overwatering, bad drainage, and low light.

☀ **SAVE IT** *Check that the pot is draining well. Repot if necessary; if the roots are rotten, remove the affected roots and surrounding soil. Do not overwater. Plants that are in darker spaces will need less water.*

SHARE THE CARE

FISH-TAIL PALM
Caryota mitis
With unusual but beautifully shaped leaves, just like fish tails. It has the same needs as the footstool palm, though it will enjoy higher humidity.

PYGMY DATE PALM
Phoenix roebelenii
A miniature date palm suitable for indoor growing, though it can still reach 6ft (1.8m). Prefers a room temperature of around 65°F (18°C).

DWARF UMBRELLA TREE
Schefflera arboricola

This leafy foliage plant is easy to grow. Keep the desired height by cutting off the top.

HOW NOT TO KILL IT

LOCATION
Place it in a reasonably warm room (55–75°F/13–24°C). Make sure it doesn't fall below 55°F (13°C) in winter.

LIGHT
Provide bright, indirect light.

WATERING + FEEDING
From spring to fall, water when the top 1in (2–3cm) of potting mix has become dry. It doesn't mind a bit of underwatering, but won't be happy if you overwater it, as this can lead to root rot (see Plant diseases, pp.28–29). Reduce watering in winter. Feed once a month in spring and summer.

CARE
You could mist the leaves in warm weather or if the plant is in a warm room. Wipe the leaves with a clean, damp cloth from time to time to keep them free of dust.

STICKY LEAVES?

Dwarf umbrella trees are prone to scale insects—the first sign is sticky leaves, which eventually turn black and sooty. You will also see brown bumps underneath the leaves.

SAVE IT *Rub off the insects and wipe the leaves clean, removing any sooty mold. Treat the leaves with insecticide. For more information, see Plant pests (pp.24–27).*

LEAVES FALLING OFF?

This could be due to temperature fluctuations, or your plant may be in too dark a spot. You may have over- or underwatered.

SAVE IT *Check that your plant is in a warm enough spot (55–75°F/13–24°C) and has plenty of indirect light. Keep it away from cold drafts. Check your watering regimen (see left).*

ZEBRA PLANT
Aphelandra squarrosa
*Often sold in flower, a zebra
plant needs similar care,
but must be kept above
60°F (15°C) in winter.
Overwatering will cause
the lower leaves to drop.*

PLANT LEANING TO ONE SIDE?

It is leaning toward
the light.

❤ **SAVE IT** *Turn
the plant regularly or
tie it to a bamboo
cane or moss pole.*

BUG ALERT!
(see pp.24–27)

Prone to **scale insects**
and **spider mites** on
the foliage.

DROOPING LEAVES?

This is due to overwatering or
underwatering.

❤ **SAVE IT** *Check the potting mix. If it's
soggy, allow it to dry out and check for signs
of root rot (see Plant diseases, pp.28–29).
Make sure you water when the top 1in
(2–3cm) of potting mix has dried out.*

*Schefflera
arboricola*

Height: up to
5ft (1.4m)

Spread: up to
3ft (1m)

CHRISTMAS CACTUS
Schlumbergera buckleyi

Christmas cacti are forest cacti—jungle evergreens rather than desert natives. They bear flowers in winter.

HOW NOT TO KILL IT

LOCATION
Place it in a room that's 65–75°F (18–24°C). To ensure it flowers, rest twice a year in cooler temperatures (see No flowers?).

LIGHT
Provide bright, indirect light.

WATERING + FEEDING
Water when the top 1in (2–3cm) of potting mix is dry, letting any excess water drain away—don't let the plant sit in soggy soil. Water more sparingly in winter. Feed monthly in spring and summer.

CARE
Place the plant on a pebble-filled tray of water for humidity, misting the leaves twice a week when it's not in flower. Repot into a slightly larger pot every 1–2 years when the root ball has filled the pot (it likes to be snug). Add some sand to the potting mix.

BUG ALERT!
(see pp.24–27)
Prone to **mealybugs** in the nooks and crannies of stems.

NO FLOWERS?
Your plant will need a rest period in order to flower again.

SAVE IT *After flowering, place your plant in a cool, unheated room (about 55°F/12°C) for an 8-week rest period, and water less. Put it outside in summer in a shady spot, and water and feed as normal. In fall, give your plant a second rest period in a cool, unheated room, ideally where no lights will be turned on at night, for 8 weeks. Then return it to its flowering position and care for it as normal.*

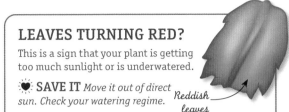

LEAVES TURNING RED?

This is a sign that your plant is getting too much sunlight or is underwatered.

❤ **SAVE IT** *Move it out of direct sun. Check your watering regime.*

Reddish leaves

EASTER CACTUS
Schlumbergera gaetneri
This species flowers in spring. Like a Christmas cactus, it likes a spell outside in summer, followed by a rest period to encourage reflowering.

Schlumbergera Hybrid

Height & spread: up to 14in (35cm)

BUDS DROPPING?

This can be caused by moving your plant when in bud, incorrect watering, or fluctuating temperatures.

❤ **SAVE IT** *Move your plant from its rest position to its regular position when in early bud, then don't move it again. Check your watering regimen (see left).*

MISTLETOE CACTUS
Rhipsalis baccifera
With the same care needs, this succulent is great for a hanging planter. Mature plants may produce fruit.

PEACE LILY
Spathiphyllum

With glossy, green leaves and occasional white flowers, this is a forgiving plant that is good for beginners.

....

HOW NOT TO KILL IT

LOCATION
Provide a warm room with a temperature of 55–80°F (13–26°C). Keep the plant away from cold drafts.

LIGHT
Place it in bright, indirect light.

WATERING + FEEDING
Water when the top 1in (2–3cm) of potting mix has become dry. Feed monthly from spring to late summer. You may need to use distilled, filtered, or rainwater if you live in an area that has hard water.

CARE
Place the plant on a pebble-filled tray of water. You could also mist the leaves once or twice a week, especially if the plant is in a warm room. Snip off any fading flowers and yellowing leaves. Repot the plant each year in spring.

BUG ALERT!
(see pp.24–27)
Prone to **mealybugs** on the undersides of the foliage.

WHOLE PLANT DROOPING?

Your plant needs water.

SAVE IT *Plunge your plant into a bucket of water for half an hour or so and allow it to drain—it should recover quickly (see Water it, pp.18–19).*

YELLOW LEAVES?

Old leaves yellow naturally. Yellowing younger leaves are a sign of stress.

SAVE IT
Check that your plant is in a good location and you are watering and feeding it correctly (see left). Repot if the root ball has filled the pot. Try switching to distilled, filtered, or rainwater.

BROWN PATCHES ON LEAVES?

This is leaf scorch.

☀ **SAVE IT**
Move your plant out of direct sunlight to a shadier position.

brown patches

SHARE THE CARE

CHINESE EVERGREEN
Aglaonema
This plant has similar care needs but can tolerate shade and temperature changes—great for a hallway.

BROWN LEAF TIPS?

This could be due to lack of humidity, or erratic watering and feeding. It could also be due to hard water.

☀ **SAVE IT** *Move away from a heat source and make sure you are feeding and watering it correctly (see left). Try switching to distilled, filtered, or rainwater.*

CAST IRON PLANT
Aspidistra elatior
Has similar care needs. Wipe the leaves occasionally, and only repot if absolutely necessary. It hates wet soil.

Spathiphyllum
Height & spread: up to 24in (60cm)

TOP 5 PLANTS FOR
YOUR LIVING ROOM

Don't relegate houseplants to a dusty corner of your living room—bring them to the fore and grow them in containers that complement your space. Here are five great plants to consider.

Snake plant
Sansevieria trifasciata

This low-maintenance favorite has a strong, architectural look that will allow it to stand out in any room. It is also a great air purifier.

See Snake plant, pp.116–117.

Fiddle-leaf fig
Ficus lyrata

This sought-after plant is a favorite of interior designers and has lush, paddlelike leaves. Don't move it after you've found the perfect spot for it, as it has a tendency to drop its leaves if moved.

See Fiddle-leaf fig, pp.76–77.

ZZ plant
Zamioculcas zamiifolia

This striking plant with its lush foliage can really create a point of interest in a room. The ZZ doesn't take up much space and is easy to grow.

See ZZ plant, pp. 138–139.

Kentia palm
Howea fosteriana

This easygoing palm will bring an air of elegance to your living room. Given good light (but avoiding direct sun), it will grow green and lush. Wipe and mist the leaves occasionally.

See Kentia palm, pp. 84–85.

Split-leaf philodendron
Monstera deliciosa

This Seventies favorite is back in fashion and is a great statement plant. Give it a bright or lightly shaded spot and plenty of space—it can grow quite large.

See Split-leaf philodendron, pp. 96–97.

BIRD OF PARADISE
Strelitzia reginae

It's easy to see how this stunning plant gets its name—the blue and orange flowers look like the head of an exotic, crested bird.

HOW NOT TO KILL IT

LOCATION
Provide warmth (at least 68°F/ 20°C) and good light. A bright bathroom or sunroom can be ideal. It also likes good air circulation, so you could put it outside in summer. It needs a minimum of around 50°F (10°C) in winter.

LIGHT
Place in as much light as possible, but keep out of direct summer sun.

WATERING + FEEDING
Water freely when the surface of the potting mix feels dry, but don't let the mix become soggy. Water sparingly in winter. Feed monthly in spring and summer.

CARE
Don't repot until the roots are visible at the top of the potting mix or are growing out of the drainage holes. Wipe the leaves with a clean, damp cloth to keep them dust-free.

NO FLOWERS?
Plants only flower after at least four years, with enough light and food, and prefer to be slightly pot-bound.

SAVE IT *Check for light levels and feeding regime, and potentially move to a smaller pot.*

BROWNING LEAVES?
There may be too little humidity, or your plant may be underwatered or overfed.

SAVE IT *Check your care regimen and that the room is not too hot and dry.*

SPLITS IN THE LEAVES?
This is completely normal. In the wild, it is an adaptation to allow air through the leaves.

BUG ALERT! (see pp.24–27)	Prone to **scale insects**, **mealybugs**, and **spider mites** on the foliage.

Strelitzia
reginae
Height: up to
6ft (1.8m)
Spread: up to
30in (75cm)

YELLOW LEAVES?

This is normal on the lower leaves of the plant—they will eventually drop off. Yellow leaves elsewhere on your plant may be due to under- or overwatering, or some aspect of its location that the plant doesn't like.

❤ **SAVE IT** *Gently pull away the yellowed leaves. Check your watering regimen and that the plant has enough light and warmth (at least 68°F/20°C).*

ROTTING AT THE BASE?

This is root or stem rot, caused by the potting mix being too wet.

❤ **SAVE IT** *Repot into fresh potting mix. Make sure the pot drains well. Don't overwater. For more information, see Plant diseases (pp.28–29).*

CAPE PRIMROSE
Streptocarpus

Cape primrose is a charming houseplant that has fresh, green leaves and pretty flowers in a range of colors.

BUG ALERT!
(see pp.24–27)

Look for **mealybugs** and **greenfly** on the undersides of the leaves.

HOW NOT TO KILL IT

LOCATION
Place in a bright room. It likes a moderate temperature of 55–70°F (13–21°C).

LIGHT
Provide indirect light. An east- or west-facing window is ideal. Keep the plant out of direct sunlight during summer.

WATERING + FEEDING
Water whenever the top 2in (4–5cm) of potting mix feels dry—aim to make the mix moist, not wet, and let any excess drain away. Reduce watering in winter. Feed every 2 weeks in spring and summer—a high-potassium fertilizer diluted by half will encourage flowers.

CARE
Repot every year in spring, into a slightly larger, shallow pot. Cut off the spent flowers to keep the blooms coming. In fall and winter, the ends of the leaves die back. This is nothing to worry about—just snip the ends off.

BROWN MARKS ON THE LEAVES?

It could be scorched or splashed with water. The ends naturally go brown in fall and winter.

🌣 **SAVE IT** *Move the plant out of direct sun. Take care not to wet the leaves when watering your plant.*

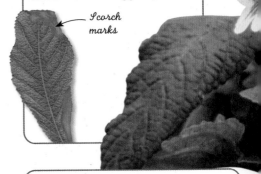

Scorch marks

LEAVES ROTTING AT THE BASE?

This may be due to overwatering, your plant sitting in water, or poor drainage.

🌣 **SAVE IT** *Remove any affected leaves and let the potting mix dry out. Check that the pot is draining excess water. Let the mix dry out between waterings.*

GRAY MOLD ON LEAVES?

This is a plant disease called botrytis.

☀ **SAVE IT** *Remove affected areas and treat with organic fungicide. For more information, see Plant diseases (pp.28–29).*

WILTING PLANT?

This is either due to over- or underwatering.

☀ **SAVE IT** *If you think you might have overwatered your plant, leave the potting mix to dry out—it needs to dry out between waterings. If you think it is underwatered, water your plant.*

GLOXINIA
Sinningia speciosa

Gloxinia has similar needs to cape primrose. Place in a bright room and keep away from drafts. It can reflower—wait for it to die back before removing any yellowed stems or leaves, and reduce watering. In spring, repot and resume watering. However, people often discard after flowering.

Streptocarpus
Height: up to 12in (30cm)
Spread: up to 18in (45cm)

LARGE LEAVES BUT FEW FLOWERS?

Your plant has been fed incorrectly, or is not getting enough bright light.

☀ **SAVE IT** *Make sure that you feed your plant every 2 weeks in spring and summer, using the correct feed. If it's in a gloomy place, move your plant to a spot with brighter, indirect light.*

AIR PLANTS
Tillandsia

In the wild, these intriguing plants grow attached to other plants. Grow them without potting mix at home, such as nestled in a glass globe or on a piece of driftwood.

HOW NOT TO KILL IT

LOCATION
A bright kitchen or bathroom can be good as an air plant likes high humidity. Don't let it get too cold (below 50°F/10°C), or expose it to drafts, especially if it is damp from watering.

LIGHT
Provide bright, indirect light. Avoid sunny windowsills as the plant may be burned by summer sun, and get too cold in winter.

WATERING + FEEDING
Water the plant by dipping and draining (see Water it, pp.18–19). Soak it for 30 minutes, or up to 2 hours if underwatered. Water about once a week in summer or when your home is heated. Use distilled, filtered, or rainwater. You can also water by misting thoroughly several times a week. Once a month, add a quarter dose of plant food to the water. Feed all year round.

CARE
After watering, shake your plant lightly and let it dry upside down for around 4 hours before returning it to its position.

NO FLOWERS?
It can take years for your air plant to be mature enough to flower.

SAVE IT *Do nothing! Some plants turn red before flowering. After it has flowered, your plant will produce "pups" (new plants at the base) and the parent plant will die.*

SOFT BROWN AREAS OR PLANT FALLING APART?
A build-up of water between the leaves has lead to rot.

SAVE IT *It's too late to save your plant. Next time, shake the plant lightly after watering and allow to drain upside down.*

CURLING LEAVES OR CRISPY LEAF-TIPS?
They are not getting enough water.

Crispy leaf-tips

SAVE IT *Water and mist your plant more regularly.*

**Tillandsia
melanocrater
tricolor**

Height & spread:
up to 1ft
(30cm)

**Tillandsia
tectorum**

Height &
spread: up to
1ft (30cm)

**Tillandsia
juncea**

Height &
spread: up to
1ft (30cm)

**Tillandsia
aeranthos**

Height &
spread: up to
1ft (30cm)

SHEDDING LEAVES?

It's normal for plants to shed some of their
outer leaves. If lots of leaves are being lost,
this is a sign that something is wrong with
your plant's environment.

💛 **SAVE IT** *Gently pull away the outer leaves.
Check that the light, humidity, and temperature
levels around your plant are correct (see left).*

INCH PLANT
Tradescantia zebrina

These unfussy, variegated plants are very easy to care for and look great in a hanging planter.

....

HOW NOT TO KILL IT

LOCATION
Place the plant in a room that is 54–75°F (12–24°C).

LIGHT
Provide bright, indirect light. It can take some direct sun.

WATERING + FEEDING
Water freely when the top 1in (2–3cm) of potting mix dries out; don't allow it to get waterlogged. Feed once a month during spring and summer.

CARE
Remove any shoots that have plain, green leaves; these grow more strongly than variegated leaves and are less attractive.

UNVARIEGATED LEAVES?
Your plant is not getting enough sunlight.

☀ **SAVE IT** Remove the unvariegated leaves and move your plant to a brighter spot.

LIMP STEMS?
The stems trail naturally, but if they look especially limp, this is probably due to underwatering or root rot, which is caused by overwatering.

☀ **SAVE IT** *Make sure you only allow the top 1in (2–3cm) of potting mix to dry out between waterings. Check for root rot (see Plant diseases, pp.28–29).*

BUG ALERT! (see pp.24–27) | Prone to **aphids** and **spider mites** on the foliage.

COLEUS
Solenostemon

Coleus, with its bright leaves, is easy to grow and has the same needs as an inch plant. If it becomes leggy, take stem cuttings.

Tradescantia zebrina

Height: up to 6in (15cm)

Spread: up to 8in (20cm)

BROWN LEAF TIPS?

The air is too dry, or your plant is suffering from a lack of water.

☀️❤ **SAVE IT** *Mist the leaves every 3–4 days. Check that you're giving your plant enough water.*

SPINDLY GROWTH OR LOSING LOWER LEAVES?

This could be due to too little light, not enough water, or not enough feed. However, it's more likely that your plant is a few years old—this plant becomes spindly with age, shedding its lower leaves.

☀️❤ **SAVE IT** Check your care regimen (see left). If your plant is old and past its best, try taking stem cuttings and repotting them to make fresh plants.

YUCCA
Yucca elephantipes

With its spiky leaves and trunk-like stems, this shrub brings a tropical touch to your home.

Whole plant

BUG ALERT!
(see pp. 24–27)

Prone to **scale insects** and **mealybugs** on the foliage.

HOW NOT TO KILL IT

LOCATION
Provide temperatures of 45–75°F (7–24°C), but not lower. A yucca is not fussy—it can tolerate fluctuations in temperature and doesn't mind dry air. Keep the plant away from children, though, as the leaves have sharp ends.

LIGHT
Place it in bright light; it can even take some direct sun. If moving your plant into direct sunlight, acclimate it gradually.

WATERING + FEEDING
Water moderately from spring to fall, whenever the top 2in (5cm) of potting mix has dried out. Water more sparingly in winter. Feed it every 2 months in spring and summer.

CARE
Wipe the leaves occasionally with a clean, damp cloth to keep them shiny and free of dust.

BENDING LEAVES?
This could be due to under- or overwatering, or some kind of shock to your plant, such as moving or repotting it.

☀ SAVE IT *Check that you allow the top 2in (5cm) of soil to dry out between waterings, and water more sparingly in winter. If you need to move your plant, move it gradually toward the new position over a week to allow it to acclimate.*

BROWN OR BLACK SPOTS ON THE FOLIAGE?
This is leaf spot, caused by bacteria or fungi.

☀ SAVE IT *Remove any affected leaves and treat with fungicide. For more information see Plant diseases (pp. 28–29).*

Black spots

YELLOWING LEAVES?

This is normal if it is only happening on the lower leaves. If it's happening all over your plant, you are probably under- or overwatering it.

♥ **SAVE IT** *Simply pull away or cut off the yellowed leaves. Adjust your watering regimen if necessary (see left).*

BROWN LEAF TIPS?

This is probably due to erratic watering.

♥ **SAVE IT** *Water your plant more frequently—when the top 2in (5cm) of potting mix has dried out.*

ROTTING STEM?

If the bark is peeling and the stem is rotting at the base, your plant has been overwatered, which is especially likely in winter.

♥ **SAVE IT** *Reduce watering and don't allow your plant to sit in cold, wet potting mix. If the problem has spread too far, you may not be able to save it.*

Yucca elephantipes
Height: up to 8ft (2.5m)
Spread: up to 3ft (1m)

SHARE THE CARE

TI PLANT
Dracaena angustifolia
The ti plant can come with bright pink, dark green, purple, lime, red, yellow, or white stripes. Prefers a higher minimum room temperature of 50°F (10°C) and will tolerate partial shade.

PONYTAIL PALM
Beaucarnea recurvata
This eye-catching tree has similar needs to a yucca. It stores water in its trunk, so be careful not to overwater.

ZZ PLANT
Zamioculcas zamiifolia

This striking, upright plant is easy to grow and doesn't mind being underwatered.

HOW NOT TO KILL IT

LOCATION
Keep the plant in a warm room (60–75°F/15–24°C) all year round. It will tolerate dry air.

LIGHT
For a lush plant, place it in bright light, out of direct sun. However, it will tolerate lower light levels.

WATERING + FEEDING
Water so that the potting mix is just moist and allow the top 2in (5cm) to dry out between waterings, all year round. Don't let the plant sit in wet potting mix. Feed once a month from spring to late summer.

CARE
Wipe the leaves with a clean, damp cloth to keep them looking shiny and to allow enough light to reach them.

> **BUG ALERT!**
> (see pp.24–27)
> Prone to **mealybugs, red spider mites,** and **scale insects** on the foliage.

YELLOWING LEAVES?
Your plant has been overwatered, or is sitting in wet potting mix. This can lead to root rot.

SAVE IT *Allow the potting mix to dry out. If the plant looks very sickly, check for signs of root rot—brown, mushy roots. Remove any affected areas and repot. For more information, see Plant diseases (pp.28–29).*

DROPPING LEAVES OR COLLAPSING STEMS?
You may have shocked your plant by moving it, perhaps from a shaded to sunny spot. Alternatively, it may be too dry or too wet at the roots.

SAVE IT *Acclimate your plant gradually to a new position. Check whether the potting mix is too dry or too wet, adjusting your watering regimen accordingly.*

BROWN PATCHES ON LEAVES?

This is sunburn.

☀ SAVE IT

Move your plant out of direct sunlight.

Brown patches

SHARE THE CARE

SAGO PALM
Cycas revoluta
This ancient plant has been around since the dinosaur era. Care for it in the same way as a ZZ plant.

BRAIDED MONEY TREE
Pachira aquatica
This plant is often sold with a braided trunk and has similar care needs to the ZZ plant.

Zamioculcas zamiifolia

Height: up to 3ft (1m)
Spread: up to 2ft (60cm)

INDEX

Adiantum raddianum 86,
    105
Aechmea fasciata 32–32
aeonium 73
Aeschynanthus pulcher 34–35
African milk tree 117
African spear 47, 117
African violet 114–115
agave 39
Aglaonema 125
air plants 132–133
Alocasia x amazonica 36–37
aloe vera 38–39, 67
aluminum plant 111
amaryllis 82–83
Anthurium 40–41
Aphelandra squarrosa 121
aphids 27
aralia, Japanese 81, 107
arrowhead plant 63
Asparagus densiflorus
    'Myersii' 42–43
  A. densiflorus Sprengeri Group 43
  A. setaceus 43
asparagus fern 43
Aspidistra eliator 107, 125
Asplenium nidus 93, 106
Astrophytum ornatum 99
Aucuba japonica 81

bamboo, lucky 46, 70–71
bathrooms, plants for
    the 86–87
Beaucarnea recurvata 137
Begonia maculata 44–45
  B. Eliator Group 45
  B. rex 45

begonias
  Eliator hybrids 45
  painted-leaf begonia 45
  polka-dot begonia 44–45
Billbergia nutans 48–49
bird of paradise 128–129
bird's nest fern 93, 106
blue star fern 104–105
blushing bromeliad 46, 49
blushing philodendron 109
Boston fern 87, 93
botrytis 28
bromeliad, blushing 46, 49
bunny ears cactus 66,
    98–99
butterfly palm 85
buying plants 14–15

cacti
  Christmas cactus 122–123
  crown cactus 99
  desert cacti 66
  Easter cactus 123
  fishbone cactus 33
  mistletoe cactus 123
Calandiva 91
Calathea 50–51
cape primrose 130–131
care of plants 20–21
Caryota mitis 119
cast iron plant 107, 125
Ceropegia woodii 57
Chamaedorea elegans 85
Chinese evergreen 125
Chlorophytum comosum 'Bonnie'
    52–53
Christmas cactus 122–123

Cissus rhombifolia 53
cleaning plants 21
Clivia miniata 54–55
Codiaeum variegatum 59
cold weather 15
condition, plant 15
Crassula ovata 56–57, 66
creeping buttons 101
Cretan brake fern 105
crocodile fern 92–93
croton 59
crown and stem rot 28
crown cactus 99
Ctenanthe burle-marxii
    58–59
curly spider plant 52–53
cyclamen, florists' 60–61
Cyclamen persicum 60–61
Cycas revoluta 139

date palm, pygmy 119
desert cactus 66
desks, plants for your 46–47
dieffenbachia 62–63
Dieffenbachia seguine 62–63
Dionaea muscipula 64–65, 67
diseases 15, 21, 28–29
  see also pests
Disocactus anguliger 33
dracaena compacta 68–69
Dracaena fragrans 68–69
  D. angustifolia 137
  D. marginata 47, 69
  D. reflexa 69
  D. sanderiana 46, 70–71
drainage 16
Dypsis lutescens 85

Easter cactus 123
Echeveria 66, 72–73
elephant's ear 36–37
elkhorn fern 112–13
  regal 113
emerald fern 43
English ivy 80–81
Epipremnum 53
Euphorbia pulcherrima
  74–75
  E. trigona 117

Fatsia japonica 81, 107
Faucaria 73
feeding plants 20
ferns
  bird's nest fern 93, 106
  blue star fern 104–105
  Boston fern 87, 93
  crocodile fern 92–93
  elkhorn fern 112–113
  foxtail fern 42–43
  maidenhair fern 86, 105
  regal elkhorn fern 113
Ficus lyrata 76–77, 126
  F. benjamina 77
  F. elastica 77
figs
  fiddle-leaf fig 76–77,
    126
  weeping fig 77
fish-tail palm 119
fishbone cactus 33
Fittonia 78–79, 86
flame nettle 135
flaming Katy 90–91
flaming sword 33
flamingo flower 40–41
florists' cyclamen 60–61
flowering plants 15
footstool palm 118–119
friendship plant 111
fungus gnats 25

gloxinia 131
grape ivy 53
gray mold 28
grooming plants 21
guzmania 33
Gynura aurantiaca 79, 87

haworthia 39
heart-leaf philodendron 107
hearts on a string 57
Hedera helix 80–81
hen & chicks 66, 72–73
Hippeastrum 82–83
Howea fosteriana 84–85, 127
Hoya bella 89
  H. carnosa 87, 88–89
humidity 17
Hypoestes 79

Imperial Red philodendron
  104–105
inch plant 134–135
indoor azalea 61
ivy
  English ivy 80–81
  grape ivy 53

Japanese aralia 81, 107

Kalanchoe blossfeldiana 90–91
  K. Calandiva® Series 91
kentia palm 84–85, 127

leaf miners 25
leaf spot 29
light 17
  low light plants 106–107
lipstick plant 34–35
living rooms, plants for your 126–127
locations 17
  low light plants 106–107
  sunny spot plants 66–67
lucky bamboo 46, 70–71

maidenhair fern 86, 104
Mammillaria 66, 98–99
Maranta 51
mealybugs 27
Microsorum musifolium 92–93
mildew, powdery 28
milk tree, African 117
Mimosa pudica 92–93
miniature roses 55
missionary plant 110–111
mistletoe cactus 121
mold
  gray mold 28
  sooty mold 29
money plant 56–57, 66
monkey cups 65
monk's hood 93
Monstera deliciosa 94–95, 127
  M. adansonii 97
  M. obliqua 95
moth orchid 102–103

natal lily 54–55
Neoregelia carolinae f. *tricolor* 46, 49
Nepenthes 65
Nephrolepis exaltata 87, 93
nerve plant 78–79, 86
never-never plant 58–59

oedema 29
Opuntia microdasys 66,
  98–99
orchid, moth 102–103
Oxalis triangularis 63

Pachira aquatica 139
painted-leaf begonia 45
palms
  butterfly palm 85
  cabbage palm 137
  fish-tail palm 119
  footstool palm 118–119
  kentia palm 84–85, 127

parlor palm 85
ponytail palm 137
pygmy date palm 119
sago palm 139
peace lily 106, 124–125
peacock plant 50–51
Peperomia argyreia 47, 100–101
  P. polybotrya 101
  P. rotundifolia 101
pests 15, 21, 24–27
  see also diseases
Phalaenopsis 102–103
Philodendron
  P. erubescens 109
  P. 'Imperial Red' 108–109
  P. scandens 107, 109
philodendrons
  blushing philodendron 109
  heart-leaf philodendron 107
  split-leaf philodendron 96–97, 127
  xanadu philodendron 97
Phlebodium aureum 104–105
Phoenix roebelenii 119
Pilea peperomioides 110–111
  P. cadieri 111
  P. involucrata 'Moon Valley' 111
pink quill 49
pitcher plant 65
plastic pots 16
Platycerium
  P. bifurcatum 112–113
  P. grande 113
poinsettia 74–75
polka-dot begonia 44–45
polka-dot plant 79
ponytail palm 137
pothos 53
potting mix 14
pots 16
  when to pot on plants 22–23
powdery mildew 28
prayer plant 51
Pteris cretica 105

purple passion 79, 87
pygmy date palm 119

queen's tears 48–49

raindrop peperomia 101
Rebutia 99
red spider mites 26
regal elkhorn fern 113
Rhipsalis baccifera 123
Rhododendron simsii 61
roots 14
rot
  crown and stem rot 28
  root rot 29
rubber plant 77

sago palm 139
Saintpaulia 114–115
Sansevieria trifasciata 116–117, 126
  S. cylindrica 47, 117
Saribus rotundifolius 118–119
Sarracenia 65
scale insects 27
Schefflera arboricola 120–121
Schlumbergera buckleyi 122–123
  S. gaetneri 123
Senecio rowleyanus 57
sensitive plant 94–95
shamrock plant 62
shape of plants 14
Sinningia speciosa 131
snake plant 116–117, 126
Solenostemon 135
song of India 69
sooty mold 29
Spathiphyllum 106, 124–125
split-leaf philodendron 96–97, 127
spotted laurel 81
stem and crown rot 28
Strelitzia reginae 128–129
Streptocarpus 130–131
string of beads 57

stromanthe 51
sunlight 17
  plants for sunny spots 66–67
Swiss cheese vine 97
Syngonium podophyllum 63

temperature 15, 17
Thaumatophyllum xanadu 97
thrips 25
ti plant 137
tiger's jaw 73
Tillandsia 132–133
  T. cyanea 49
Tradescantia zebrina 134–135

umbrella tree 120–121
urn plant 32–33

Venus fly trap 64–65, 67
vine weevils 26
violet, African 114–115
viruses 29
Vriesea splendens 33

watering 18–19
watermelon peperomia 47, 100–101
wax flower 87, 88–89
wax plant, miniature 89
weeping fig 77
whiteflies 25
wilting 19

xanadu philodendron 97

yucca 136–137
Yucca elephantipes 136–137

Zamioculcas zamiifolia 127, 138–139
zebra plant 121
ZZ plant 127, 138–139

ABOUT THE AUTHOR

Veronica Peerless is a trained horticulturalist and garden designer and an experienced writer and editor. She is currently commissioning content editor at *Gardens Illustrated*, having previously worked as a content producer at gardenersworld.com and as deputy editor at *Which? Gardening*. She has contributed to publications including *The English Garden*, *Garden Design Journal*, and *Telegraph Gardening*. She was horticultural consultant on *The Gardener's Year*, also published by DK.

ACKNOWLEDGMENTS

Author: Many thanks to Christian King for his support and endless cups of tea while I was writing this book.

Publisher: DK would like to thank houseofplants.co.uk for allowing photography of their plants—African spear, blushing philodendron, butterfly palm, croton, Easter cactus, fiddleleaf fig, Guinea chestnut, guzmania, horsehead philodendron, Indian rope plant, kentia palm, lucky bamboo, mistletoe cactus, parlour palm, snake plant, song of India, ZZ plant, and several other plants that didn't make the final version of the book. The photo of the Calandiva was taken by Katherine Scheele Photography.

First Edition 2017
Editor Toby Mann
Senior Art Editor Alison Gardner
Designers Rehan Abdul, Karen Constanti
Managing Editor Dawn Henderson
Managing Art Editor Marianne Markham
Publishing Director Mary-Clare Jerram

Picture credits: The publisher would like to thank the following for their kind permission to reproduce their photographs:
(Key: a-above; b-below/bottom; c-center; f-far; l-left; r-right; t-top)

44–45 Dreamstime.com: Andreadonetti (c). **53 Dreamstime.com:** Slyadnyev Oleksandr (l). **100 Dreamstime.com:** Olga Miltsova (crb). **118–119 Shutterstock.com:** AHatmaker (c)

All other images © Dorling Kindersley

For further information see:
www.dkimages.com

TOXICITY

Some houseplants are toxic to humans and pets and can be hazardous if they are ingested or come into contact with the skin or eyes. For information about which plants are toxic, please visit:

www.rhs.org.uk
www.aspca.org